The Shipwrecked Mind

The Shipwrecked Mind
On Political Reaction

Mark Lilla

NEW YORK REVIEW BOOKS

New York

THIS IS A NEW YORK REVIEW BOOK
PUBLISHED BY THE NEW YORK REVIEW OF BOOKS
435 Hudson Street, New York NY 10014
www.nyrb.com

Financial support was made possible by the French government and managed through
the "Investissements d'avenir" program of the Agence Nationale de la Recherche
(ANR-11-LABX-0027-01 Labex RFIEA+).

Library of Congress Cataloging-in-Publication Data
Names: Lilla, Mark, author.
Title: The shipwrecked mind : on political reaction / by Mark Lilla.
Description: New York : New York Review Books, [2016] | Series: New York
review books
Identifiers: LCCN 2016011770 | ISBN 9781590179024 (paperback)
Subjects: LCSH: Political science—Philosophy. | Political psychology. |
Religion and politics. | BISAC: SOCIAL SCIENCE / Sociology of Religion. |
PHILOSOPHY / Essays. | PHILOSOPHY / Religious.
Classification: LCC JA71 .L55 2016 | DDC 320.01—dc23
LC record available at https://lccn.loc.gov/2016011770

ISBN 978-1-59017-902-4
Available as an electronic book; ISBN 978-1-59017-903-1

Printed in the United States of America on acid-free paper
1 3 5 7 9 10 8 6 4 2

To A.S. and D.L.
compagnons de route

Contents

Introduction

THE SHIPWRECKED MIND

*To the eyes that have dwelt on the past, there is no
thorough repair.*

—George Eliot

WHAT IS REACTION? Consult any decent university library
and you will find hundreds of books in all the world's major
languages on the idea of revolution. On the idea of reaction
you will be hard put to find a dozen. We have theories about
why revolution happens, what makes it succeed, and why,
eventually, it consumes its young. We have no such theories
about reaction, just the self-satisfied conviction that it is
rooted in ignorance and intransigence, if not darker motives.
This is bewildering. The revolutionary spirit that inspired
political movements across the world for two centuries may
have died out, but the spirit of reaction that rose to meet it
has survived and is proving just as potent a historical force,
from the Middle East to Middle America. This irony should
pique our curiosity. Instead it arouses a kind of smug outrage

that then gives way to despair. The reactionary is the last remaining "other" consigned to the margins of respectable intellectual inquiry. We do not know him.

The term "reaction" has an interesting history. It first entered the vocabulary of European political thought in the eighteenth century, when it was taken over from the scientific treatises of Isaac Newton. In his highly influential work *The Spirit of the Laws* Montesquieu portrayed political life in dynamic terms as an endless series of actions and reactions. He recognized revolution as one such political act, but considered it rare and unforeseeable. One revolution might transform a monarchy into a democracy, another might turn a democracy into an oligarchy. There was no way of predicting the outcome of revolutions, or the kind of reactions they might provoke.

The French Revolution changed the meaning of both terms. No sooner had the revolt broken out in Paris than observers began developing stories that would make the Revolution the pivot of world history. The Jacobins reset the calendar to Year I to mark the break, and for good measure renamed all the months so that no citizen would confuse past and present. All previous history took on meaning as a preparation for this event, and all future action could now be oriented toward history's predetermined end, which was human emancipation. What would political life then look like? Hegel thought it would mean the establishment of modern bureaucratic nation-states; Marx imagined a communist nonstate populated by freemen who would fish in the morning, raise cattle in the afternoon, and criticize after dinner. These differences were less important, though, than their confidence in the inevitability of arrival. The river of time flows in one direction only, they thought; reversing upstream is impossible. During the Jacobin period anyone who resisted the river's flow or displayed insufficient enthusiasm about reaching the destination was labeled a "reactionary." The term acquired the negative moral connotation it still retains today.

Over the course of the nineteenth century, though, it became apparent that not all critics of the Revolution were reactionaries in the precise sense. Reformist liberals like Benjamin Constant, Madame de Staël, and Tocqueville judged the collapse of the ancien régime to have been unavoidable, but not the Terror that followed, which meant that the promise of the Revolution might still be redeemed. Conservatives like Edmund Burke rejected the radicalism of the Revolution but especially the historical myth that subsequently developed around it. Burke considered the idea of history as an impersonal force carrying us to fixed destinations to be both false and dangerous, since it could be used to justify crimes in the name of the future. (Liberal and socialist reformers had an additional worry, which was that it would encourage passivity.) History, for Burke, develops slowly and unconsciously over time, with results no one can predict. If time is a river, then it is like the Nile delta, with its hundreds of tributaries branching out in every imaginable direction. The trouble starts when rulers or ruling parties think they can anticipate where history is already headed. This was illustrated by the French Revolution itself, which instead of ending European despotism had the immediate unintended consequences of putting a Corsican general on an imperial throne and giving birth to modern nationalism—outcomes no Jacobin foresaw.

Reactionaries are not conservatives. This is the first thing to be understood about them. They are, in their way, just as radical as revolutionaries and just as firmly in the grip of historical imaginings. Millennial expectations of a redemptive new social order and rejuvenated human beings inspire the revolutionary; apocalyptic fears of entering a new dark age haunt the reactionary. For early counterrevolutionary thinkers like Joseph de Maistre, 1789 marked the end of a glorious journey, not the beginning of one. With astonishing speed the solid civilization that was Catholic Europe was reduced to a magnificent shipwreck. This could not have been an accident. To explain it Maistre and his many progeny became adepts at telling a sort of horror story. It recounted, often melodramatically, how centuries of cultural and intellectual developments culminated in the Enlightenment, which rotted the ancien régime from within, so that it broke to pieces the moment it was challenged. This story then became the template for reactionary historiography in Europe, and soon around the world.

Post hoc, propter hoc is the reactionary's profession of faith. His story begins with a happy, well-ordered state where people who know their place live in harmony and submit to tradition and their God. Then alien ideas promoted by intellectuals—writers, journalists, professors—challenge this harmony and the will to maintain order weakens at the top. (The betrayal of elites is the linchpin of every reactionary story.) A false consciousness soon descends on the society as a whole as it willingly, even joyfully, heads for destruction. Only those who have preserved memories of the old ways see what is happening. Whether the society reverses direction or rushes to its doom depends entirely on their resistance. Today political Islamists, European nationalists, and the American right tell their ideological children essentially the same tale.

The reactionary mind is a shipwrecked mind. Where others see the river of time flowing as it always has, the reactionary sees the debris of paradise drifting past his eyes. He is time's exile. The revolutionary sees the radiant future invisible to others and it electrifies him. The reactionary, immune to modern lies, sees the past in all its splendor and he too is electrified. He feels himself in a stronger position than his adversary because he believes he is the guardian of what actually happened, not the prophet of what might be. This explains the strangely exhilarating despair that courses through reactionary literature, the palpable sense of mission—as the reactionary American magazine *National Review* put it in its very first issue, the mission was to "stand athwart history, yelling Stop!" The militancy of his nostalgia is what makes the reactionary a distinctly modern figure, not a traditional one.

It also explains the enduring vitality of the reactionary spirit even in the absence of a revolutionary political program. To live a modern life anywhere in the world today, subject to perpetual social and technological change, is to experience the psychological equivalent of permanent revolution. Marx was only too right to remark how all that is solid melts into air and all that is holy is profaned; he was only mistaken to assume that the abolition of capitalism alone could restore weight and sanctity to the world. The reactionary comes closer to the truth in his historical myth-making when he blames modernity *tout court*, whose nature is to perpetually modernize itself. Anxiety in the face of this process is now a universal experience, which is why anti-modern reactionary ideas attract adherents around the world who share little except their sense of historical betrayal. Every major social transformation leaves behind a fresh Eden that can serve as the object of somebody's nostalgia. And the reactionaries of our time have discovered that nostalgia can be a powerful political motivator, perhaps even more powerful than hope. Hopes can be disappointed. Nostalgia is irrefutable.

The mind of the modern revolutionary has been the subject of great literature. But the reactionary has yet to find his Dostoevsky or Conrad.* The retrograde, sexually repressed

---

*The great exception is Thomas Mann. His character Leo Naphta in *The Magic Mountain* is a brilliant creation: a tubercular Jewish convert to Catholicism

cleric, the sadistic right-wing thug, the authoritarian father or husband are familiar cartoons in our literature and visual culture. Their ubiquity is a sign of imaginative laziness of the B-movie kind that puts sheriffs in white hats and bandits in black ones. But the engaged political reactionary is driven by passions and assumptions no less comprehensible than those of engaged revolutionaries, and develops theories no less sophisticated to explain the course of history and to illuminate the present. It is nothing but a prejudice to assume that revolutionaries think while reactionaries only react. One simply cannot understand modern history without understanding how the reactionary's political nostalgia helped to shape it, or make sense of the present without recognizing that as a self-declared exile he, no less than the revolutionary, can sometimes see it more clearly than those who feel at home in it. We owe it to ourselves to understand his hopes and fears, his assumptions, his convictions, his blindness, and, yes, his insights.

The Shipwrecked Mind makes a very modest start. It is the fruit of my own aleatory reading over the past two \

---

who became a Jesuit priest, only to develop sympathies for communism that could just as well have been for fascism. Naphta is driven to a kind of intellectual hysteria by nostalgia for the Middle Ages and the conviction that modern history has gone terribly off course. Only a violent revolution reestablishing absolute authority can redeem mankind, he believes. That Mann modeled this character on the Marxist philosopher and revolutionary Georg Lukács shows how well he understood the affinities between the revolutionary and the reactionary. That Lukács failed to recognize Mann's sketch shows how little he understood himself.

decades and offers a series of examples and reflections rather than a systematic treatise on the concept of reaction. For some time I have been trying to better understand the ideological dramas of the twentieth century by studying how certain exemplary intellectual figures were swept up into them. In 2001 I published *The Reckless Mind*, which gathered some portrait-essays I had done on thinkers who seduced themselves into supporting or discounting the realities of modern tyrannies like Nazi Germany, the Soviet Union, China, and the theocratic Republic of Iran.* My hope was to shed some light on what I called tyrannophilia, the narcissistic attraction of intellectuals to tyrants who they imagine are translating their own ideas into political reality.

While working on that book I began to notice a different force that shaped the imaginations of political thinkers and ideological movements in the twentieth century, and that was political nostalgia. Nostalgia settled like a cloud on European thought after the French Revolution and has never fully lifted. It became particularly potent in the aftermath of World War I, which prompted an "end of civilization as we know it" despair hardly different from what opponents of the Revolution felt after 1789. That anguish only intensified after World War II, the revelation of the Shoah, and the deployment of nuclear weapons and their subsequent proliferation. This string of disasters cried out for explanation. And so a crowd of thinkers—philosophers, historians, theologians

---

* *The Reckless Mind: Intellectuals in Politics* (New York Review Books, 2001).

—began to offer them. First was Oswald Spengler in his hugely influential study *The Decline of the West* (1918–1923). A host of competing declinists followed his example, all claiming to have discovered the decisive idea or the decisive event that sealed our doom. Since the 1950s this has been a popular and growing literature on the European and American right. But its tropes can also be found on the fringe left, where apocalyptic deep ecologists, antiglobalists, and anti-growth activists have joined the ranks of twenty-first-century reactionaries. In a less well known story, traces of Spengler's historical mythmaking also appear in the writings of radical political Islamists, whose story of the secular West's decline into decadence, and the inevitable triumph of a vigorous, renewed religion, has European fingerprints all over it.

The Shipwrecked Mind opens with essays on three early-twentieth-century thinkers whose work is infused with modern nostalgia—Franz Rosenzweig, Eric Voegelin, and Leo Strauss. Rosenzweig was the least explicitly political of the three. A German Jew who began as a scholar of Hegel's political writings, he abandoned philosophy on the eve of World War I to devote the rest of his short life to the revitalization of Jewish thought and practice. His was a complex nostalgia. He was convinced that the failure of Judaism to find a place in modern European society derived in part from an attempt to reform itself according to modern notions of historical progress, which were rooted in Christianity. But he did not believe that a return to simple, premodern Orthodoxy was possible or even desirable. What he proposed was a "new thinking" that would turn its back on history in order to recapture the vital transcendent essence of Judaism. "The battle against history in the nineteenth-century sense," he wrote, "becomes for us the battle for religion in the twentieth-century sense."

The essays on the philosophers Voegelin and Strauss form a pair. Both left Europe in the 1930s and made very successful careers after the war in the United States, where they acquired ardent followings. They, like many of their contemporaries, thought it urgent to explain the collapse of democracy and the rise of totalitarianism in terms of a calamitous break in the history of ideas, after which intellectual and political decline set in. In his voluminous writings on religion and politics, Voegelin eventually settled on ancient religious gnosticism as the force that set the West on its disastrous course. Strauss developed a subtle and much deeper account of the history of Western philosophy, built up from careful studies of thinkers from Plato to Nietzsche. In his view, Machiavelli was responsible for the decisive historical break within the philosophical tradition, turning it from pure contemplation and political prudence toward the willful mastery of nature. Though their accounts of Western intellectual history were incompatible, they both helped to shape the historical imagination of American intellectuals on the right. This episode is not without its ironies. For in learning how to tell a story that idealizes a lost America—and then blames European ideas for destroying it—they unknowingly reproduce a very European cultural pessimism. A perfect example

is *The Closing of the American Mind*, the popular book by
Strauss's student Allan Bloom, where after chapters about the
destructive power of European nihilism one finds the confident declaration that "whether it be Nuremberg or Woodstock, the principle is the same."

After these portraits I consider two contemporary intellectual movements whose rhetoric also traffics in nostalgia,
though to very different ends. I begin with theoconservatism,
a prominent strain on the American right that brings together traditional Catholics, evangelical Protestants, and
neo-Orthodox Jews who despite doctrinal differences share
a sweeping condemnation of America's cultural decline and
decadence, for which they blame reform movements within
these denominations and what they perceive as secular attacks on religion more generally. Their attention tends to focus on the "Sixties" as the significant break in American
political and religious history, but more ambitious theocons
have looked much further back, even to medieval Catholic
theology, to locate where the slippery slope began. I then turn
to a small but intriguing movement on the academic far left
that focuses on religion from a very different perspective. Its
proponents cast a nostalgic gaze on revolutionary movements
of the past, and sometimes even on the totalitarian states of
the twentieth century. What they share is a fascination with
"political theology" and its most prominent theorist, the former Nazi legal scholar Carl Schmitt.* Having given up on

---

* See the chapter on Schmitt in *The Reckless Mind*.

the Marxist theory of history and its deterministic materialism, but rejecting the post-1989 neoliberal consensus, they now conceive of revolution as a theological-political "event" that reveals a new dogma and imposes a new order in defiance of the apparent drift of history. There are deep affinities in their eyes between Saint Paul, Lenin, and Chairman Mao.

What follows these chapters is an essay about a single event: the deadly terrorist attacks by French-born jihadists that took place in Paris in January 2015. I happened to be living there at the time and was struck by the encounter of two forms of reaction in the incident and its aftermath. On the one side was the nostalgia of the poorly educated killers for an imagined, glorious Muslim past that now inspires dreams of a modern caliphate with global ambitions. On the other was the nostalgia of French intellectuals who saw in the crime a confirmation of their own fatalistic views about the decline of France and the incapacity of Europe to assert itself in the face of a civilizational challenge. The entire affair was reminiscent of the period between the two world wars, when an anxious cultural pessimism shared across the political spectrum was fed by the reality of political violence and fantasies about the catastrophic course of history.

The Shipwrecked Mind concludes with a meditation on the enduring psychological power of political nostalgia, beginning with the tragicomic quest of Don Quixote to revive the Golden Age. Political nostalgia reflects a kind of magical thinking about history. The sufferer believes that a discrete Golden Age existed and that he possesses esoteric knowledge of why it ended. But unlike the modern revolutionary whose actions are inspired by a belief in progress and imminent emancipation, the nostalgic revolutionary is unsure how to conceive of the future and act in the present. Should he simply withdraw and become an inner emigrant, a secret resister? Should he lead the charge back to the past in all its glory? Or should he strive for a future that will be an even more glorious version of it? Don Quixote grapples with all these possibilites. His personal quest has as much to teach us about the ideas and passions behind the collective political dramas of our time as any learned analysis of social, economic, and cultural forces. We seem to have forgotten that such forces only have force once they are filtered through the subjective outlooks of human beings, the ideas and images they use to make sense of things. The more charmed we have become with our individual psyches, the less adept we have become at understanding the psychology of nations, peoples, religions, and political movements. That the present has become so illegible to us is in no small measure due to this imbalance. *The Shipwrecked Mind* was conceived as a small contribution to correcting it.

Thinkers

THE BATTLE FOR RELIGION

Franz Rosenzweig

The Second Temple was not like the First.

—John Dryden

FRANZ ROSENZWEIG WAS born on Christmas Day 1886 into an assimilated Jewish family in Kassel, Germany. Although there was a long tradition of religious learning in the family, Franz acquired only a superficial introduction to Jewish life at home, where the Sabbath was not celebrated. His family hoped he would pursue a medical career but at the University of Freiburg his interests shifted to philosophy and modern history under the influence of the distinguished scholar Friedrich Meinecke, who supervised his doctoral dissertation. A gifted student, Rosenzweig gave every appearance of being a conventional academic in the years leading up to World War I.

Privately, though, he was preoccupied by religious and philosophical questions that scholarship could not help him address. A number of his close Jewish friends and relatives had converted to Christianity, though not for the usual social reasons. In the early years of the twentieth century a Kierkegaardian mood settled on German intellectual life, a sense that political unification, the flowering of a wealthy bourgeois culture, and the triumph of the modern scientific outlook were extinguishing something essential that could only be recaptured through some sort of religious leap. The title of one of the most influential books of the time captured the mood perfectly: *The Holy: On the Irrational in the Idea of the Divine and Its Relation to the Rational* (1917), by the Protestant theologian Rudolf Otto. Rosenzweig felt this draw toward the beyond and was particularly taken with his friend Eugen Rosenstock-Huessy, a Jewish convert to Christianity who would later have a career as a historian in the United States. In discussions and letters Rosenstock-Huessy tried to convince him that Christianity was, historically speaking, the final and most complete religion. And so, in the summer of 1913, Rosenzweig announced his intention to convert as well, telling his astonished mother that the New Testament was true and that "there is only one way, Jesus."

What happened next is now part of legend. Before converting to Christianity, the story goes, Rosenzweig decided to attend Yom Kippur services one last time, and there he experienced what might be called a preemptive counterconversion, deciding on the spot to devote himself to Judaism. That, in any case, was the account Rosenzweig's mother gave. He himself never wrote about the incident and it is doubtful he would have described such a melodramatic, quasi-Christian awakening. Still, we know from his letters that something important did happen in the fall of 1913, making it possible for him to write to one of his converted cousins, "I have reversed my decision. It no longer seems necessary to me, and therefore, being what I am, no longer possible. I will remain a Jew."

Rosenzweig was as good as his word. That fall he began to meet with the eminent neo-Kantian philosopher Hermann Cohen, who after his retirement from the University of Marburg taught philosophy at a Jewish institute in Berlin, where Rosenzweig was studying Hebrew and Talmud. He also met Martin Buber, who would become a lifelong friend and collaborator, and began writing essays on the nature of Judaism. When the war broke out Rosenzweig was sent to an antiaircraft unit on the Macedonian front, which was relatively quiet. That left him time to pursue his studies and even to meet some Sephardic Jews, whose lives of simple piety deeply impressed him. While in Macedonia Rosenzweig also began work on a book to be called *The Star of Redemption*, which was an exercise in what he called "the new thinking" and offered a persuasive if idiosyncratic account of Jewish experience. Notes for the book were copied onto postcards that he mailed back to his mother for safekeeping, and it was from these that he reconstructed and published the book after the war.

In 1920, while working on an edited version of *The Star*, Rosenzweig was called to Frankfurt to become the director of a new Jewish studies center, the Freies Jüdisches Lehrhaus, one of the most important sites of the short-lived Jewish re-awakening of the Weimar years. He also brought his first life to an end by publishing his dissertation on Hegel's theory of the state, an essential study that is still consulted today. His teacher Meinecke was so pleased with it that he offered Rosenzweig a university lectureship, but was turned down. In a vivid letter to the baffled Meinecke, Rosenzweig explained how the spiritual crisis of 1913 had put his life under "a 'dark drive' which I'm aware that I merely *name* by calling it 'my Judaism.'" From that point on the pursuit of knowledge seemed to him increasingly vain unless put in the service of flesh-and-blood individuals seeking a way to live. And when *The Star of Redemption* was published the next year to few and generally uncomprehending reviews, Rosenzweig took it stoically. The center of his life was no longer even Jewish thought, it was the renewal of Jewish life itself.

The Frankfurt study center was open between 1919 and 1926. Its teachers and students, ranging from future scholars of Judaism to secular thinkers like Erich Fromm and Leo Strauss, were put through a rigorous program meant to lead them from their assimilated lives back to a direct encounter with the sources of the Jewish tradition without the mediation of modern philosophy or reformed theology. Yet no sooner had this worthy effort begun than Rosenzweig fell ill with a degenerative condition, amyotrophic lateral sclerosis (Lou Gehrig's disease), which doctors said would kill him within the year.

Defying their predictions he lived another seven years,

producing a steady current of essays, reviews, and translations under the most arduous conditions imaginable. He first wrote on a specially equipped typewriter; when his muscles failed he communicated with his wife by blinking as she passed her finger over a board with the alphabet on it. In this manner, without ever leaving his apartment again, he managed to translate the poems of the medieval thinker Judah Halevi, as well as, with Buber, the first ten books of the Hebrew Bible. He died in December 1929 in Frankfurt, where his gravestone still stands.

In his private diaries Rosenzweig dropped a curious remark that turns out to offer a key for entering his thought. "The battle against history in the nineteenth-century sense," he wrote, "becomes for us the battle for religion in the twentieth-century sense." What does it mean to battle against history? And what is religion—and Judaism in particular—"in the twentieth-century sense"?

For Rosenzweig and his intellectual generation in Germany, "history" meant the philosophy of history, which in turn meant Hegel. Throughout the nineteenth century, Hegel had been understood, correctly or not, as having discovered a rational process in world history that would culminate in the modern bureaucratic state, bourgeois civil society, a Protestant civil religion, a capitalist economy, technological advances, and Hegel's own philosophy. This was the prophecy. But as it seemed to be approaching fulfillment near the end of the nineteenth century, horror set in and a deep cultural reaction followed in Germany and in other countries where Hegel's ideas were influential. Expressionism, primitivism, fascination with myth and the occult—a Pandora's box of movements and tendencies was opened. The horror was genuine: if Hegel and his epigones were right, the whole of human experience had been explained rationally and historically, anesthetizing the human spirit and foreclosing the experience of anything genuinely new, personal, or sacred. It meant, in Max Weber's chilling phrase, "the disenchantment of the world."

Whether or not this is what Hegel intended, it certainly is how he was understood, even within the German philosophical establishment, which took seriously his claim to have brought the history of philosophy to a rational end. The rebellion against this claim took many forms. Some anti-Hegelians, hoping to reestablish the independence of thought from history, promoted a return to earlier thinkers like Kant or even Descartes. Others took a more subjective path, turning to Nietzsche or the existential paradoxes of Kierkegaard, who was just being translated into German at the end of the century. These turns, accompanied by a growing sense that Hegel's historical consciousness had brought the entire culture to a crisis of relativism, then bore fruit in the phenomenological works of Edmund Husserl and the young Martin Heidegger. Rosenzweig would come to share Heidegger's conviction that from its very inception philosophy had made an error by turning away from what Rosenzweig called "the everyday of life" and had lost itself in what Heidegger called "metaphysics." And this error could only be rectified through a new kind of therapeutic thinking that would return human beings to ordinary experience.

Rosenzweig's call to a "battle for religion in the twentieth-century sense" was also directed against Hegel, although the more proximate target was the liberal schools of theology that had dominated German religious thinking throughout the nineteenth century. Liberal theology, represented by figures like David Friedrich Strauss and Friedrich Schleiermacher, began as an attempt to work out a compromise between the doctrines of Protestant Christianity and modern thinking, and in this effort Hegel proved a useful ally. Hegel did not share the French Enlightenment view that religion was mere superstition; nor did he believe that it would be extinguished by the modern conquest of nature. He thought that Protestantism and the modern state were in fact fundamentally harmonious and that even with the culmination of history religion would continue to serve a quasi-bureaucratic function, helping to reconcile individuals to the state through moral and civic education. The leading German Protestant theologians of the nineteenth century, still bruised from the Enlightenment's attacks, were willing to accept this limited but secure position in the Hegelian scheme.

Odd as it may seem today, many Jewish thinkers in the nineteenth century aspired to the same position. The emancipation of Germany's Jews at the beginning of the century had brought with it the creation of a new intellectual discipline, free from the closed traditional world of rabbis and yeshivas, called the "science of Judaism" (*Wissenschaft des Judentums*). The aims of this discipline were reformist and apologetic. By demythologizing those aspects of Judaism that erected cultural barriers against the entrance of Jews into the current of modern life, liberal Judaism hoped to enlighten the Jewish people and make them more acceptable to Christian fellow citizens. Hegel's insistence that only Protestantism, as the most mature form of religious experience, was compatible with modern life was, in their view, just a detail. Once the fundamental moral teachings of Judaism, separated from the dross of superstition and tradition, were shown to be virtually identical to those of Protestantism; once modern Jews became fully participating citizens of a modern state; once, as Hermann Cohen infamously put it, the spiritual harmony of *Deutschtum* and *Judentum* was allowed to develop—then, liberal Jews reasoned, the Protestant prejudice would be forgotten and Judaism's place in the modern firmament would be assured.

By the early decades of the twentieth century the theological-political illusions of liberal theology were only too apparent to the most thoughtful Protestants and Jews. After the disaster of World War I the young Swiss pastor Karl Barth wrote an explosive book called *The Epistle to the Romans* that threw into doubt everything liberal Protestantism stood for—humanism, enlightenment, bourgeois culture, the state. Barth's call to smash the idols and make an existential decision, against the modern spirit and for a suprahistorical faith, changed Protestant thought forever. Rosenzweig's place in modern Jewish thought is similar to Barth's among Protestants, with one important difference. While Barth believed that a return to the basic faith of Saint Paul and the Reformers was both necessary and possible, Rosenzweig never for a moment considered returning intellectually to any sort of Orthodox Judaism. For him—and, he believed, his entire generation—this was impossible. A century of assimilation had produced Jews so spiritually atrophied that they could no longer be Jews in a full sense without some sort of inner transformation. The problem of contemporary Jewish education, Rosenzweig wrote in 1924, was to determine "how 'Christian' Jews, national Jews, religious Jews, Jews from self-defense, Jews from sentimentality, loyalty, in short, 'hyphenated' Jews such as the nineteenth century has produced, can once again, without danger to themselves or Judaism, become *Jews*." Given the damage done by theological liberalism, only a "hygiene of return" could fully renew the Jewish people.

The notion of return is what links Rosenzweig's two-front battle, against history and for religion. Modern philosophy, which reached its culmination in Hegel's philosophy of history, had cut man off from life and alienated him from what is most his own. Modern liberal theology, whether Christian or Jewish, had gone further by alienating him from his God, whose commands had been reduced to the level of good citizenship and bourgeois propriety. If man was to return to himself and his God, if he was to learn to live fully again, he would have to undergo some sort of therapy: not by moving back in time but by learning to escape it. That therapy is what Rosenzweig's writings aimed to provide.

It is understandable that readers hoping to understand Rosenzweig turn first to *The Star of Redemption*, his magnum opus. Few get very far into it, though, for that mystical, seven-sealed work does little to explain Rosenzweig's therapeutic intent. A better way to begin is to consult a little book that he wrote (but never published) to introduce his ideas to a wider public, and that has been translated into English as *Understanding the Sick and the Healthy.** This is a small masterpiece of German philosophical prose, at once playful and profound. The conceit is that it is a medical report, written to ordinary readers over the heads of "experts," concerning a patient who falls ill and must be cured—the illness being philosophy itself. Before taking to his sickbed the patient went about his business in the flow of life, occasionally wondering about this or that, but eventually putting wonder aside to get on with the commonsensical business of living. One day, though, he was unable to leave his wonder alone and stopped dead in his tracks;

---

*The German title—*Das Büchlein vom gesunden und kranken Menschenverstand*—contains a play on words difficult to translate into English. *Gesunder Menschenverstand* can be literally translated as "healthy human understanding" but actually means "common sense." In the title Rosenzweig wanted to contrast common sense to an intellectual malady for which there is no handy term. A clumsy translation that captures the contrast might be "The Booklet on Common Sense and Unhealthy Thought."

the continuous flow of life started to pass him by. Rather than thoughtlessly use simple words like "cheese," he began to reflect: "What is cheese *essentially*?" Cheese became an "object" for him and he became the "subject," and a nest of philosophical problems was opened. Soon the poor man was no longer able to eat cheese, or anything at all. His common sense had been crippled by a stroke and he was paralyzed.

Is there a cure for such an illness? From the Stoics to Montaigne to Wittgenstein there is a stream of Western philosophy that conceives its mission in therapeutic terms as releasing minds from pointless or destructive reflection and returning them to the flow of life. But Rosenzweig believed that this was not as simple as leading a fly out of a bottle. Common sense, like unreflective religious faith, is lost if challenged, and once lost must be actively restored. In his story the cure begins when the patient is taken on an orchestrated trip to the countryside outside the sanatorium. The vista is dominated by three separate peaks, which Rosenzweig calls God, man, and world. When a philosopher encounters these land masses his first instinct is to burrow into them to discover their common properties. In different historical periods philosophers have declared the hills to be made entirely of God (pantheism), entirely of man (idealism), or entirely of world (materialism), but they have never succeeded in finding a fourth substance. That, Rosenzweig conjectures, is because there is none: there just *are* three elements out there.

From week to week, as the patient moves from one peak to the next, he is reacquainted with these elements in their integrity; and at the end of the three-week cure, he is finally able to see God, man, and world for what they are, self-sufficient but related to one another within the whole of existence. Once that happens he is able to use ordinary language again without wondering what is behind it. As part of his convalescence he is returned home but is put on a strict schedule akin to a religious calendar, which allows him to experience life again within an ordered annual cycle. The patient's legs get reaccustomed to moving through the flow of time and he starts to live in the moment, yet also anticipates his death with tranquillity. Socrates believed that only philosophy could teach us how to die; Rosenzweig's patient faces mortality by purging himself of the philosophical urge.

This is a beautiful allegory. But the question still remains: Why did Rosenzweig think that the path out of the philosophical tradition could—and for him must—lead back to Judaism?

To answer this question we must turn to *The Star of Redemption*—and immediately our way is blocked. Rosenzweig's short writings, direct and engaging, are like printed invitations to return to common sense and begin a new kind of thinking and living. *The Star*, by contrast, is an eccentric philosophical system written, if not in the high nineteenth-century style, then certainly in competition with the old masters. At a time when Heidegger and Wittgenstein were already breaking philosophically and stylistically with the German system-builders, Rosenzweig tried one last time to outdo Hegel. It was a fateful mistake. For generations now the genuine philosophical and religious insights of his book have been buried within a web of theosophical-cosmological speculations, distracting neologisms, and a pastiche of borrowed notions regarding thought, time, and language that Rosenzweig insisted constituted a "new thinking." But once one penetrates beyond what one critic called *The Star*'s "Kabalistic symbol-mongering," one discovers a profound meditation on what it would mean to live a life at once fully reconciled to human finitude and open to the experience of transcendence (or "redemption") within it.

The interplay of finitude and transcendence is the theme of the second part of *The Star*. Here Rosenzweig speaks of the relations among God, man, and world in terms of "creation," "revelation," and "redemption," terms to which he gives special meaning. All religions, including pagan ones, see the world and human beings as creatures of the gods. What distinguished Judaism, Rosenzweig says, and following it Christianity and Islam, was the discovery that such a world is mute and unfinished unless it is quickened through reciprocal human and divine activity. God and man encounter each other in the moment of revelation and are transformed miraculously by it, as is the world. The language of their meeting is that of love. In a beautiful exposition of the Song of Songs, Rosenzweig describes a living God who to become more fully himself develops concern for His creation, infusing it with love. Man feels himself to be the object of this affection and is transformed in turn, permitting a genuine encounter through speech. The whole of creation now has an "orientation," Rosenzweig says, and man above all.

Love reveals, but it also wants to fulfill. It wants, in Rosenzweig's terms, to redeem, to make God, man, and world whole and perfect. But how is this redemption to happen? Orthodox Christianity and Judaism place it at the end of time when God wills it, while modern thinkers like Schelling and Hegel imagined that creation was being brought to perfection through the workings of an immanent principle. Rosenzweig's conception of redemption combines these orthodox and heterodox notions in a unique, if not altogether coherent, way. He accepts the orthodox teaching that ultimate redemption can only take place outside time and is brought about by God alone, not by some anonymous world-soul permeating everything. But he also says that we "anticipate" redemption in the present, preparing the world and ourselves for an ultimate reckoning that we can only hope for, not hasten. And while we wait, love continues to do its work as we live and worship together. By making this human interaction possible, God is preparing His own eventual redemption (a very old gnostic idea).

As Rosenzweig remarks, the doctrine of redemption is a breeder of heresies. The problem is deep: if redemption is wholly God's work, we are tempted to leave Him to his work and ignore our own; if, however, we participate in this redemptive labor, the temptation is equally great to think we can redeem ourselves through temporal activity. Rosenzweig sees a kind of wisdom hidden beneath these heresies and offers an ingenious explanation of them. He suggests that behind them lie two complementary but equally valid ways of living in the light of revelation and awaiting redemption. One way belongs to Judaism, the other to Christianity.

The third part of *The Star of Redemption*, and by far the richest, is a startling sociological comparison of Jewish and Christian ways of life. (Rosenzweig dismisses Islam as a mere parody of revealed religion.) His portrayal of Christianity is dramatic if not wholly original, deriving as it does from Hegel. For Rosenzweig as for Hegel the distinguishing theological mark of Christianity is belief in the incarnation of God in Jesus Christ and the expectation of His return. This revelatory event had the consequence, though, of dividing time into three periods: the eternal age before Christ's arrival, the eternal age of redemption that will follow His return, and the temporal epoch in which Christians must live, and which Rosenzweig calls the "eternal way." Sociologically speaking, this means that Christianity is and is meant to be a force in history.

The manner in which Christians understand their revelation and await redemption turns their individual and collective lives into a journey. The Christian is always en route, making his way from pagan birth to baptism, overcoming temptation, spreading the Gospel; and so is the Church, which considers all men brothers and therefore feels obliged to convert them or, if necessary, conquer them. Because he is an eternal pilgrim, Christian man is alienated, feeling himself divided, as Rosenzweig vividly puts it, between Siegfried and Christ, and is therefore never fully at home in the world. Yet this tension in the Christian soul was highly productive. Struggling with itself, Christian culture moved the waves of history forward, out of antiquity into the medieval world, then to the centuries of Protestantism, and finally to the modern age when, by being secularized, Christianity triumphed. In this way, Christianity prepares the redemption of the world through activity in time. (It bears reminding that this was Hegel's, not Saint Augustine's, view of Christian destiny.)

Judaism answers a different call, according to Rosenzweig. Long before the revelation of Christianity and the opening of its history, the Jews, as the sole people of revelation, lived in a timeless, face-to-face relationship with their God. They needed no mediator because they already had a direct rapport with the Father; they were given no historical task because they were already what they were destined to be. Rather than work toward redemption in time, the Jews anticipate redemption in symbolic form through their religious calendar, and in this sense already live an eternal life. "The Jewish people," Rosenzweig wrote, "has already reached the goal toward which the [other] nations are still moving," which means that for them history itself has no meaning. "Only the eternal people, which is not encompassed by world history, can—at every moment—bind creation as a whole to redemption while redemption is still to come." Even while living in their own land, the Jews are always in exile—from history.

Jewish isolation from the rest of humanity is maintained through divine law and the Hebrew language, but its strongest defense is blood ties. Rosenzweig's remarks on Judaism as a blood religion have embarrassed some readers, and even the English translator of *The Star* lightly bowdlerized them. Yet there is nothing ignoble in what Rosenzweig had to say. The only way for a religious community to master fortune and guarantee a direct, continuous, and eternal relation with God is for it to be a "blood-community." "All eternity not based on blood," Rosenzweig notes, "must be based on the will and on hope. Only a community based on common blood feels the warrant of eternity warm in its veins even now....The natural propagation of the body guarantees it eternity." The Jews did not strike root in land, as the pagans did, or in history, as the Christians would; they struck root in themselves as a way of vouchsafing their eternal relationship with God. Christians attest to their faith by proselytizing strangers whom they consider brothers. The Jews attest by reproducing, by saying through the body that "there shall be Jews," and thereby renewing the covenant between generations past and future. This does not mean that Jews are morally indifferent to the plight of other peoples, only that their concern grows out of love for God and each other, not out of devotion to an abstraction called humanity.

Perhaps the most imaginative pages of *The Star* are devoted to an analysis of the Jewish religious calendar, in
which Rosenzweig sees an infinitely rich set of rituals struc-
turing symbolically how the Jewish people experience creation, revelation, and redemption. He sees a kind of divine
drama in the structure of the Sabbath day, in the family fes-
tivals from Pesach to Sukkot, and in the communal holidays
from Rosh Hashanah to Yom Kippur. The entire cycle of
human existence is found reproduced here in every year of
Jewish life. This is the common sense of Judaism, the living
link between God, man, and world that traditional philosophy cannot understand.

This common sense comes at a price, however. It is that
the Jews, as the bearers of divine law on earth, must for-
swear a life of politics. Rosenzweig follows Hegel closely
here in seeing law as a synthesis of custom and reason, developing in time, and the state as a concrete expression of law.
And since Jews consider the divine law to be immutable (if
open to infinite interpretation), it follows, according to
Rosenzweig, that there cannot be a Jewish state, and any
messianic attempt to found one is idolatrous. "The state," he
writes, "symbolizes the attempt to give nations eternity
within the confines of time," thus making it a rival of the
eternal people that has already attained eternity. The Jews
simply cannot take politics, and especially war, seriously;
they are a nation of prophets, perhaps on occasion of utopian dreamers, but definitely not a nation of politicians and
generals. Because they are in transcendental exile from his-

tory, they are transcendentally stateless. Needless to say, Rosenzweig was not a Zionist.

There are, then, two peoples awaiting their final redemption. Individual Christians focus on spiritual rebirth, every moment finding themselves at the crossroads of decision; as a people they are oriented toward the future, radiating their message out into the pagan darkness and appropriating whatever is lit there. Individual Jews, on the other hand, live as links in a chain of generations running backward and forward; their rebirth happens communally as they procreate, as they guard memory of the past, and as they internalize their spiritual existence. A slightly chauvinistic tone enters *The Star* now and again as Rosenzweig contrasts the psychological and social harmony of Jewish life with the self-alienation at the root of Christianity's creative destruction. In the end, though, he sees them as complementary ways of life, each fulfilling a function in the economy of redemption.

By complementarity Rosenzweig did not mean that, in order to be itself, Judaism somehow needs Christianity; it does not. But the world, it seems, does. As early as 1913, not long after his aborted conversion to Christianity, Rosenzweig expressed the view that Judaism "leaves the work in the world to the church and recognizes the church as the salvation for all heathens in all time." Jews do not proselytize but it is good that Christians do. Christianity, on the other hand, needs Judaism if it is to perform this function: while it is busy converting the pagans without, the example of Judaism helps Christians to keep at bay the pagan within. "If the

Christian did not have the Jew at his back," Rosenzweig asserts, "he would lose his way." Christians are aware of this, too, and hence resent the Jews, calling them proud and stiff-necked. The very existence of Judaism and its claim to have experienced eternity shames the pilgrim Christians, who become anti-Semites out of self-hate, out of disgust with their own pagan imperfections.

Rosenzweig was no ecumenical utopian. He knew that Jew and Christian could never agree on ultimate matters if they took themselves seriously. God "has set enmity between the two for all time," he wrote, and once remarked in a letter, "We have crucified Christ and, believe me, we would do it again, we alone in the whole world." Yet God in his wisdom also bound the two religions together for as long as time will last. Judaism and Christianity are imperfect ways of experiencing revelation and redemption because they are human ways. Rosenzweig likens the Jews to a people that sees the light but is unable to live in it temporally, while Christians live in an illuminated world but cannot see the light itself. The whole truth about God, man, and world— whatever that truth might be—eludes both peoples. It is in their limitations, not their achievements, that Judaism and Christianity find common ground.

The last sentence of *The Star of Redemption* reads quite simply: "*Ins Leben*"—"Into life." And that, in the end, is its therapeutic aim: to prepare readers for leaving behind the illusions of the "old thinking" and entering fully into what Rosenzweig calls *das Nichtmehrbuch*, the no-longer-book that is life itself. What that would mean for Christians is clear enough: it would mean accepting their fate as a historical people and learning to see the modern, secularized world as the sanctified fruit of Christian revelation and not, as Barth would have it, as the serpent's fruit. For Jews it would mean turning away from history as the locus of redemption or even temporal fulfillment. They would live in relation to the past but only in the sense that each Jewish holiday reenacts an old drama that bears more relation to eternity than to time.

Rosenzweig's nostalgia turns the Jewish past into a transcendental ideal rather than a state to be recovered by moving back in time. It is a beautiful ideal, though steeped in pathos. For a few years after Rosenzweig's death, politics would catch up with the Jews of Europe and block every exit. It left them no choice but to plunge back into history's flow and seize control of their destiny, for the first time since antiquity. For the Jewish people since the Shoah, building a future out of the present has of necessity become *das Leben*. Eternity must wait.

THE IMMANENT ESCHATON

Eric Voegelin

The historian is a backward-looking prophet.
—Friedrich von Schlegel

CRISIS IS THE mother of history. Beginning with Herodotus the urge to write history has been bound up with the need to explain the seemingly inexplicable reversals of fortune suffered by nations and empires. The best histories satisfy that need while still capturing the openness and unpredictability of human action, though the best histories are not always the most memorable. Historians who offer "multicausal explanations"—and use phrases like that—do not last, while those who discover the hidden wellspring of absolutely everything are imitated and attacked but never forgotten.

In the twentieth century, European history writing became a kind of *Trümmerliteratur*, a look back at the rubble of a civilization that collapsed in 1933 ... or 1917, or 1789, or further back still. Germans have specialized in this kind of literature of ruins, and not only because so much debris litters the German landscape. In the nineteenth century, historians wanted to imitate Hegel, whose grand philosophical vision wove together every aspect of human culture into a seamless dialectical account of historical progress. After the catastrophe of World War I the challenge was to transform that story into an apocalyptic one of rupture and decay with philosophical meaning. Oswald Spengler was not alone. Edmund Husserl spoke for many German thinkers when he declared, in a famous lecture just before World War II, that "the 'crisis of European existence'...becomes understandable and transparent against the background of the *teleology of European history* that can be discovered philosophically."

For reasons of its own, America has rarely cultivated crisis history, despite the apocalyptic streak in our native religious imagination. But when German scholars fleeing Hitler began arriving in the United States in the 1930s, they imported some very large and very dark ideas about the crisis of the age, which then found resonance here. Though the diagnoses of Hannah Arendt, Leo Strauss, Max Horkheimer, and Theodor Adorno were very different, they all assumed that it was transformations in Western thinking that had prepared the unthinkable, and that a new intellectual path had to be found before a political one could be.

For much of his adult life, Eric Voegelin was among them. An Austrian émigré who was on friendly terms with both Arendt and Strauss, Voegelin never acquired a wide public readership in his lifetime. There are academic Voegelinians in North America and Europe, but Voegelin himself was too solitary and idiosyncratic a thinker to leave behind a proper school. He was an original, a hothouse flower transplanted from the dark garden of German *Geschichte* to the land of the open road. Which was why, in the end, his historical nostalgia did not survive the assault of his limitless curiosity.

Eric Voegelin was born in Cologne in 1901 and left Germany for Vienna when he was nine. He was trained in law and political science but his real education, he later said, came from reading Karl Kraus, the acerbic Viennese journalist whose attacks on the hypocrisy and vulgarity of his time shaped the generation coming of age around World War I. Voegelin's detachment from his Austrian homeland prepared him to take an unusual step for a young European academic. In 1924 he traveled to the United States on a fellowship and spent two years studying in American universities, attending the courses of John Dewey at Columbia and discovering the works of George Santayana. This experience inspired his first book, *On the Form of the American Mind* (1928), which owes more to German thinkers like Max Scheler and Wilhelm Dilthey than to American pragmatists like Dewey. Still, Voegelin's American experience had large effects. When he returned to Vienna to accept a university appointment, he brought with him an abiding hatred of racism and the shameful intellectual justifications of it. After pseudoscientific works supporting the Nazis' biological racism began circulating in Austria, he attacked them in two books published not long after Hitler seized power. These and other of his writings made him a choice target of Austrian Nazis, who ordered his arrest immediately after the *Anschluss* in 1938. He escaped by train while the police searched his apartment.

Though neither a Communist nor a Jew, Voegelin found himself among the mass of émigré scholars seeking work and safety in the United States. Despite his previous American experience, unheard of in this group, he had trouble finding a position teaching American government because he was a German-speaking foreigner. He finally ended up at Louisiana State University, where he taught until 1958, and began writing books in English. On the basis of these works he was invited back to Germany to establish a research institute in Munich, where he stayed for ten years until the poisonous political atmosphere of the late 1960s drove him away. (He was stuck, as he once put it, "between the staid dummies of tradition and the apocalyptic dummies of revolution.") He returned to the United States in 1969, taking a position at the Hoover Institution in California, and died there in 1985.

Voegelin was astonishingly productive during his American years, but in an odd way. Shortly after arriving he was asked by an American publisher to do a short history of political thought to compete with other standard textbooks in the field, and he began writing an enormous, unfinished manuscript called *History of Political Ideas*, which takes up eight of the thirty-four volumes of *The Collected Works*. After abandoning it as too unwieldy in the 1950s, he then launched a projected six-volume study of "order and history" that also remained unfinished at his death. On top of these undertakings Voegelin produced hundreds of reviews and essays, several more books, extremely long and involved letters, interviews, and a charming short autobiography. Such logorrhea, and in a foreign tongue, inspires amazement. And suspicion, too.

A first glance at Voegelin's works leaves the unprepared reader baffled, since they seem to be about everything—Byzantine history, medieval theology, gestalt psychology, Paleolithic and Neolithic visual symbols, Greek philosophy, American constitutional development, the Dead Sea Scrolls, Chinese imperial history, Old Testament interpretation, Polynesian decorative arts, Zoroastrianism, Egyptian and Mesopotamian cosmology, Renaissance images of Tamerlane, and much else. He brings to mind George Eliot's Mr. Casaubon from *Middlemarch*, the obsessive polymath whose search for the "key to all mythologies" left him only torsos of unfinishable works. But guiding all Voegelin's writing was a basic intuition about the relation between religion and politics, and how transformations in that relation could explain the cataclysms of modern history.

The germ of all Voegelin's major works is to be found in *The Political Religions*, a dense pamphlet dashed off just before the *Anschluss*, which had to be published in Switzerland after he fled. In it he attacked the Nazis as children of darkness, though he blamed the modern secular West for making

Nazism possible. This was, to say the least, an unusual perspective, since the modern secular West was just then gearing up for war against Hitler. To make his case, Voegelin sketched out a story that he would elaborate and refine over the next three decades.

The story begins with the early civilizations of the ancient Near East, in Egypt and Mesopotamia, where states were endowed with a divine aura giving them legitimacy. In that lost world the king was presented symbolically as representative of the divine order, serving either as an intercessor with the gods or as a god himself. For Voegelin, this was the original condition of all civilizations, which could not have established an order without believing in its sanctity. The bond between the divine and the human was a tight one in the ancient world and only loosened with the rise of Christianity, which was the first world religion to offer theological principles for distinguishing divine and political orders.

Though those principles were honored mainly in the breach, as Voegelin recognized, the very idea of distinguishing a transcendent City of God from a terrestrial City of Man had deep spiritual and political implications for Western history. On the one hand, it opened up paths to God that did not have to pass through the royal palace; on the other, it raised the prospect of human beings governing themselves without direct divine guidance. Spiritual enrichment came with the risk of political impoverishment, and eventually with the temptation to free man entirely from divine supervision. The radical Enlightenment of the seventeenth and eighteenth centuries willingly succumbed to that temptation, completing the work begun by Christianity: in Voegelin's words, it "decapitated God."

Yet the modern liberation of politics from God did not mean the liberation of man from man. Quite the contrary. Though the Enlightenment banned God from the city, it could not abolish the practice of divinization that had originally given rise to civilization. What happened in modern Western history after the Enlightenment, in Voegelin's view, was that human beings began to conceive in sacred terms their *own* activities, in particular their creation of new political orders free from traditional sources of authority. Modern man became a Prometheus, believing himself a god capable of transforming anything and everything at will. "When God has become invisible behind the world," Voegelin said, "the things of the world become new gods." Once this is understood, the true nature of the mass ideological movements of the twentieth century—Marxism, fascism, nationalism—becomes evident: they were all "political religions," complete with prophets, priests, and temple sacrifices. When you abandon the Lord, it is only a matter of time before you start worshiping a Führer.

This hydraulic notion, of a religious drive that reappears in secular life if it is denied access to the divine, has been a staple of Counter-Enlightenment thinking since the nineteenth century, especially among Christian theologians protesting the course of modern history. But those theologians had a clear remedy in mind: return to the one true faith. Was this Voegelin's remedy as well? It was not—though reticence about his own religious views led more than a few of his conservative readers to think it was. Voegelin, who was raised a Protestant, wrote casually about the "transcendent" or "divine" as if its existence were unquestionable, but he never expressed any particular doctrinal faith about it and was openly critical of Christianity, which he blamed for preparing the advent of modern politics. Instead, he wrote about the history of religion and philosophy as the story of man's repeated attempts to make sense of what lies beyond the temporal sphere and to determine its relation to individual consciousness and the social order. Though we cannot know anything about Voegelin's private beliefs, he clearly valued the power of religion itself as a vitalistic force shaping human society that could be directed to good ends so long as its proper function was respected. He left no doubt that he accepted in his own way the existence of a divine transcendent order. The basic theme of *The Political Religions* is that the fantasy of creating a world without religion, a political order from which the divine was banned, led necessarily to the creation of grotesque secular deities like Hitler, Stalin, and Mussolini.

It is also the theme of *The New Science of Politics* (1952), Voegelin's first book in English, and of the grand, multivolume work he called *Order and History*, which began appearing in 1956. Fresh from the experience of the war and the destruction caused by the "political religions," Voegelin wanted to develop a new political science that would analyze the symbols by which all societies conceive of themselves and order their institutions in history. His concept of "symbol" was somewhat vague, but also flexible, allowing him to compare, for example, the symbolism of ancient Mesopotamian kingship to that of American democratic rhetoric. It is, of course, an anthropological commonplace that aspects of political life—such as the crowning of a king, the architecture of palaces and assemblies, the rituals of voting—have symbolic meaning. What was novel in Voegelin's thought was how he wedded that commonplace to a theory of history, suggesting that a universal process of symbolization was surreptitiously at work in human civilization, giving world history a discernible direction.

This process could be revealed, he thought, once we see every society as a "cosmion," a self-contained imaginative world invested with meaning and believed to match the structure of a transcendent order. Take, for example, the preamble to the ancient Babylonian Code of Hammurabi, which Voegelin cites:

When Anu the Sublime, King of the Anunaki, and Bel, the lord of Heaven and earth, who decreed the fate of the land assigned to Marduk, the over-ruling son of

> Ea, God of righteousness, dominion over earthly man, and made him great among the Igigi, they called [the land of] Babylon by his illustrious name, made it great on earth, and founded an everlasting kingdom in it, whose foundations are laid so solidly as those of heaven and earth; then Anu and Bel called by name me, Hammurabi, the exalted prince, who feared God, to bring about the rule of righteousness in the land, to destroy the wicked and the evil-doers; so that the strong should not harm the weak; so that I should rule over the black-headed people like Shamash and enlighten the land, to further the well-being of mankind.

Here the structure of the "everlasting kingdom" is compared straightforwardly to that of the cosmos ("Heaven and earth"), and the prince's dominion over his people likened to the gods' dominion over "earthly man."

Sometime in the first millennium BCE, Voegelin asserted, this symbolic order became more complex, more "articulated." Man and society began to be viewed independently of each other, and both as needing philosophy or revealed religion to bring them into alignment with divine order. The true man was now one who worked to bring about that harmony in his own soul, and the true ruler was one who tried to achieve it in society. A whole new set of symbols was developed to reflect this outlook, which reached its greatest clarity in ancient Athens. In this "golden hour in history," as Voegelin called it, the philosophy of Plato and the dramas of

Aeschylus expressed the newly revealed truth about human existence.

Voegelin's sweeping view of the development of civilization owed much to the mystical speculations on the "ages of man" of the German philosopher Friedrich Schelling in the nineteenth century, and to Spengler, Arnold Toynbee, and Karl Jaspers in the twentieth. He did something new, though, when he made his story revolve around the phenomenon of gnosticism. "Gnosticism" is a term that has meant many things to many people over the centuries. Coined in the anti-heretical literature of the early Church, it was used to tar different heterodox groups that had sprung up in late antiquity, some claiming to be Christian, others Jewish. These groups were thought to share three basic beliefs: that the created world was the work of an evil lower deity, or demiurge, and thus utterly corrupt; that direct access to a higher, spiritual divinity was possible for those with a secret knowledge (*gnosis*) developed from a divine spark within; and that redemption would come through a violent apocalypse, led, perhaps, by those possessing *gnosis*. Today an enormous scholarly literature exists on these sects, and also on whether they shared much at all.

A narrow subject, it might seem. But in fact the concept of gnosticism has played a large role in German thought ever since the early nineteenth century, when theologians and biblical scholars clashed over whether gnosticism was at the root of Christianity. Soon this academic controversy turned into a very public debate over the degree to which even modern thought was indebted to heterodox and heretical religious ideas of the ancient world. Already in the 1830s Hegel was being attacked as a modern gnostic, and the charge was soon leveled against the utopians and revolutionaries who came after him. This polemic was revived after World War II when the German Jewish scholar Hans Jonas published an influential study called *The Gnostic Religion.* As a young student of Heidegger, Jonas was drawn to ancient gnosticism by what he thought were religious anticipations of the philosophical truths expressed in his teacher's early existentialism. After the war, and after Heidegger's public embrace of Nazism, Jonas developed a much darker view of the gnostic impulse and how it affected politics. His final judgment on Heidegger's thought was that it expressed a "modern nihilism infinitely more radical and more desperate than gnostic nihilism ever could be."

Voegelin's argument in *The New Science of Politics* was now that the entire modern age, which grew out of a rebellion against Christianity, was gnostic in nature. Christianity had advanced beyond the symbols of the Greek world, articulating the notion that although individuals are products of nature and society, they are also direct children of God whose lives are aimed ultimately toward salvation. This double nature of man was Christianity's great revelation—and its secret weakness, since it cast human beings into a hostile world with a divine mission (as Franz Rosenzweig had also

believed). The life of the Christian pilgrim is hard, his progress slow. It offers no solace on earth, certainly not in political life, which is subordinated to the spiritual mission of the
Church and is bound up with our fallen nature. And human
beings are impatient: told that salvation awaits them, they
rush ahead, building towers up to Heaven or hastening the
Apocalypse. Gershom Scholem had discovered similar dy-
namics in Jewish mysticism, but in Voegelin's eyes they
reached the highest intensity in Christianity, whose messiah
had already arrived, then inexplicably departed. And so, at a
certain point, European Christians got tired of waiting;
lacking "the spiritual stamina for the heroic adventure of the
soul that is Christianity," they rebelled and decided to build
their paradise on earth, using their own powers. This was
how the modern age was born, through a gnostic "imma-
nentization of the Christian eschaton"—that is, the pursuit
of the millennium in the political here and now.

This is the idea for which Voegelin was best known in his
lifetime, and it earned him many admirers among those
American conservatives who saw a "crisis of the West" in
the cold war, in mass popular culture, in the student rebel-
lions—in just about everything. By dismissing Hegel and
Marx as gnostic prophets, "petty paracletes in whom the
spirit is stirring," Voegelin gave world-historical reasons for
dismissing them and their epigones. The histories of modern
political revolutions, of liberal progressivism, of technological advance, of communism, of fascism—what were they but
testimonies to gnostic rebellion against the very idea of a

transcendent order? That Voegelin thought Christianity was partially to blame for this rebellion, and that the American Revolution was one result of it, somehow escaped his conservative readers. In 1968 he published a short, dyspeptic book called *Science, Politics, and Gnosticism*, in which he called modern gnostics the "murderers of God," Marx an "intellectual swindler," and all modern mass political movements forms of "ersatz religion." The American translation was a hit and has remained in print at conservative publishing houses ever since.

Shortly after the appearance of *The New Science of Politics* Voegelin published in rapid succession the first three volumes of *Order and History*, which began tracing the entire arc of civilization, starting with the ancient Near East and running down to the present. This was conceived less as a survey than as a rational reconstruction of the process by which the symbolization of human experience had become increasingly articulate up until the birth of Christianity, and then had declined owing to modern gnosticism. These early volumes offer a brilliant if eccentric ride through ancient history, beginning with Mesopotamia, Egypt, and Israel, then taking up the Greek story, from the Cretans and Achaeans down to classical Athens. They are not embarrassments. Voegelin was an earnest amateur historian who seemed to have read everything and could make connections among myths, inscriptions, urban planning, zodiacs, prophecies, epic poetry, biblical stories, Greek tragedies, and Platonic dialogues. His first three volumes quickly established the human ascent up to Christianity, and his cold war American readers looked forward to reading about their own civilizational decline.

Then something happened: Mr. Casaubon changed his mind.

It was seventeen years before another volume of *Order and History* appeared, during which time Voegelin spent a decade building his German research institute. When it was finally published in 1974 his readers discovered that he had renounced much that he had written. Up until that point, Voegelin's works were like those of other antimodern cultural pessimists who since the nineteenth century have constructed historical narratives presuming to pinpoint the moment when healthy modes of thinking and living were abandoned and the rot began. For Heidegger it began with Socrates, for Strauss with Machiavelli, and for Voegelin, at least until then, it began with ancient gnosticism. But the fourth volume of *Order and History*, titled *The Ecumenic Age*, opens with the startling confession that his original historical schema had fallen prey to the very impulse he had criticized, the "monomaniacal desire to force the operations of the spirit in history on the one line that will unequivocally lead into the speculator's present." Now he had come to realize that history is "a mystery in the process of revelation," an open field where the divine and human meet, not a highway without exits. For centuries mystics had tried to express this truth in hermetic language that left the mystery unexplained. What was needed, Voegelin now declared, was an objective, scholarly discipline for discovering the truth of this "theophanic" encounter without robbing it of its fundamental mystery. That now became the program of *Order and History*.

Alas, the last two volumes of this work are very tough going, not least because Voegelin felt the need to develop a specialized vocabulary all his own, using terms like "eristics," "metaleptic consciousness," "metastatic faith," "pneumatic theophany," and "egophanic history," as if they were transparent. (The final volume of *The Collected Works* has a thirty-eight-page glossary to help the reader navigate it all.) And there is a regrettable elephantiasis, as the writing veers from lists of Sumerian kings to Max Weber, from Saint Paul to Mircea Eliade, from Xerxes to Jacob Burckhardt, from the Shang dynasty to Rudolf Bultmann. A reader unfamiliar with these epochs and writers will make nothing of it. Which is a pity, since his basic intuition was a deep one.

Voegelin first tried to express it in an unusual book he published in Germany called *Anamnesis* (1966), and which was translated into English only a decade later. It begins not with the problem of history but with the problem of memory—in Greek, *anamnesis*. What is it about consciousness, Voegelin asks himself, that makes us conceive of our experience in terms of beginning and end, rupture and continuity? And how does that psychological proclivity affect the way we construct our societies? He was now convinced

that "the problems of human order in society and history"—
including the problem of gnosticism—"originate in the order
of consciousness." In the 1940s he even began his own private "anamnetic experiments," as he called them, in which
he explored his childhood memories and tried to recover
the emotions at their core, reflecting on how such feelings
might have shaped the construction of his own past. His
strange but suggestive notes on these experiments are included in the book. But the guiding thought behind it all is
that the human and transcendent realms meet in human
consciousness, an old mystic notion that Voegelin extends to
history, suggesting that through us "eternal being realizes
itself in time."

When this odd and stimulating book appeared in Germany, Voegelin confessed to a friend that it had affinities
with the hermetic writings of Plotinus and the medieval text
The Cloud of Unknowing, and that he was trying to master
a "new literary form in philosophy." He never did. In his final works this poetic impulse lies etherized on the table of
scholarship. Nor did he satisfy his cold war American readers, who, after a seventeen-year wait, hoped to find in the
final volumes of *Order and History* more ammunition for
their battle against modern progressivism. One conservative
critic wrote in a review that "the hope of Christian conservatives" had become "a latter-day Pilate." Voegelin was amused
by the American need to pigeonhole him, remarking in his
autobiography that in his long career he had been called a
Catholic, a Thomist, a Protestant, a Hegelian, a Platonist,

"not to forget that I was supposedly strongly influenced by Huey Long."

Universal histories teach us more about the historical crises that inspire them than they do about the civilizations they describe. Those hoping to understand how the shock of the two world wars shaped subsequent European and American thought have much to learn from Voegelin's grand narratives, whose ambitions, however imperfectly realized, gave measure to the felt enormity of the twentieth-century disaster. And those concerned with the revival of political messianism in our time would do well to consider his searching reflections on the gnostic impulse. But it was perhaps his willingness to question publicly his own motives and assumptions, to abandon certain fixed ideas and revise others, that has the most to teach us today. It takes a good deal of self-awareness and independence of mind to renounce the bittersweet comforts of cultural pessimism and question the just-so narratives of civilizational decline that still retain their allure for Western intellectuals. Eric Voegelin was many things—an American traveler, a critic of racism, an amateur historian, a mythologist, a system-builder, an explorer of human consciousness, a mystic. But beneath all that *Wissenschaft* he was also something Dorothea Brooke never found in her poor Mr. Casaubon: a free spirit.

ATHENS AND CHICAGO

Leo Strauss

Ancient Greece is the most beautiful invention of
the modern age.

—Paul Valéry

LEO STRAUSS WAS born into a rural Jewish family outside Marburg, Germany, in 1899. His boyhood ambitions, he once remarked, were simple and pastoral: to become a country postman, raise rabbits, and read Plato. His family was observant but not educated, and after serving in World War I he drifted into Zionist circles and began writing for their political publications. Strauss studied philosophy in several German universities, eventually writing his dissertation under Ernst Cassirer in Hamburg. The encounter that left the most lasting impression, though, was with Martin Heidegger, whose lectures Strauss attended in Freiburg and Marburg. He belonged to a privileged generation of then young Jewish students—including Hannah Arendt, Hans Jonas, Karl

Löwith, and Herbert Marcuse—who encountered Heidegger just as he was becoming himself as a thinker.

In the early 1920s Heidegger began giving courses on ancient philosophy that were anything but conventional. Rather than simply explicate the views of Plato and Aristotle, he wanted to expose and question their most basic assumptions—in particular their ontological assumptions about "what is." His intuition was that the first philosophers had distorted this question and that something had been lost, that a way of thinking and even of being in the world had been abandoned in the effort to give a rational account of what is. This radical questioning is what drew students like Strauss to him. Expecting to meet a professor, they encountered a thinker.

At the time, it was unclear where Heidegger was going with this questioning. It would be some years before he made his way back to the pre-Socratic thinkers who, he argued, had given priority to the "question of Being"—that is, the question of what it means "to be," not what or how things are. And it would be longer still before he articulated his fundamental thought: that once Plato began to talk about the "Ideas" and Aristotle began talking about "essences," there was a "forgetting of Being" that would have enormous consequences for Western civilization. We fatefully departed from an original "dwelling" with Being and embarked on a path that eventually led to the conquest of nature by science and technology and the self-alienation of mankind. Today we live inauthentically. Not, as Rousseau and the Romantics would have it, because we lost our original innocent goodness; nor, as Catholic reactionaries would have it, because we abandoned the Church; nor, as Marx would have it, because of the rise of capitalism. We live inauthentically because of Socrates.

There was only one Heideggerian, and that was Heidegger. But all the students of Strauss's cohort were marked by his dual questioning of the philosophical tradition and modern life. Löwith was drawn away from philosophy toward religion and theology; Marcuse threw himself into Marxism and political action. Arendt brought this spirit of questioning to modern politics and history, and Jonas brought it to gnosticism and the modern natural sciences. Strauss was a case apart. He was never an official student of Heidegger's, and perhaps for just that reason took up Heidegger's challenge more directly than the others did. He was to devote his intellectual life to the defense of Socratic philosophy, or at least "the possibility of philosophy." On his account, the trouble in Western civilization began when early-modern and Enlightenment thinkers turned away from the Greek tradition and tried to reestablish philosophy and politics on new foundations.

This was anything but a scholastic disagreement. Heidegger's view of a decisive historical break in Western thought reflected and fed his apocalyptic view of modernity and his nostalgia for earlier modes of life more in harmony with nature. That nostalgia eventually inclined him to join the Nazi Party, out of the illusion, incomprehensible today, that fascism would restore mankind's rapport with Being.* Heidegger's philosophical influence only grew after the war, yet his historical vision and political views no longer convinced anyone but himself.

Strauss's legacy was double. Though he neither sought nor attained Heidegger's stature as a philosopher, the influence of his thinking about the "quarrel between the ancients and moderns" continues to spread, particularly in Europe and Asia. But it was in the United States, where he spent his entire teaching career, that the political implications of his historical narrative of loss were developed. And in ways he could not have anticipated, it helped to reshape American politics at the end of the twentieth century. Though the story of Heidegger's philosophical rise and political fall is one of the most dramatic episodes in modern intellectual history, his thinking has had no perceptible influence on Western political life. The thinking of Leo Strauss, the self-effacing student at the back of the classroom, has.

Philosophy, for Heidegger and Strauss, was haunted by a doppelgänger. For Heidegger it was the open-ended "thinking of Being" that the pre-Socratics practiced and that some great poets, like Hölderlin, captured in verse. For Strauss, the doppelgänger was divine revelation. On his telling, the hidden wellspring of Western civilization and the source of

---

*On Heidegger and his involvement with National Socialism, see my *The Reckless Mind*, chapter 1.

its vitality was a tension between two incompatible ways of addressing the human condition.

The oldest, which appears in all civilizations, is to seek guidance through divine revelation; the other, which was developed in ancient Greece, was to seek it exclusively through human reason. This tension was already apparent in Greek life but became much more intense in late antiquity with the encounter between the biblical tradition of revelation and Greek philosophy. From that point on starkly different ways of thinking and living presented themselves to reflective people, one idealized in Athens and the life of Socrates, the other in Jerusalem and the life of Moses. And between them, one had to choose.

Why must one choose? Because, Strauss held, all societies require an authoritative account of ultimate matters—morality and mortality, essentially—if they are to legitimate their political institutions and educate citizens. Theology has traditionally done that by convincing people to obey the laws because they are sacred. The philosophical alternative to this obedience was Socrates's life of perpetual questioning beholden to no theological or political authority. For Strauss this tension between Athens and Jerusalem was necessary and in any case inevitable in human society. Without authoritative assumptions regarding morality and mortality, which religion can provide, no society can hold itself together. Yet without freedom from authority, philosophers cannot pursue truth wherever it might lead them.

In one sense, this is a tragic situation, as the execution of

Socrates for impiety and the persecution of philosophers by religious authorities over the centuries show. But in another, it is a healthy one, since the philosopher and the city each have something to teach the other. Philosophers can serve as gadflies to the city, calling it to account in the name of truth and justice; and the city reminds philosophers that they live in a world that can never be fully rationalized, with ordinary people who cling to their beliefs and need assurance. The wisest philosophers, in Strauss's estimation, were those who understood that they must be political philosophers, thinking about the common good. But they must also be politic philosophers, aware of the risks they take in challenging false certainties.

In his early writing Strauss developed a distinctive take on this "theological-political problem" and its relation to the modern Enlightenment. In his view, the Lumières, horrified by the Wars of Religion and frustrated by the otherworldliness of classical philosophy, wanted to create a new kind of society that would be free of both religion and classical philosophy—of Athens *and* Jerusalem. On the one hand, they mocked religion and wanted to crush it, rather than simply distance or protect themselves from it. On the other, they redirected philosophy's attention away from contemplation of the true, the beautiful, and the good, and toward more practical ends. The monument to this reorientation was the French *Encyclopédie*. The assumption behind it was that the world could be reformed on the basis of reason and empirical inquiry. And that assumption, on Strauss's reading of modern history, was wrong. All the Lumières managed to do was distort philosophy's mission, leaving it and the world worse off. Philosophy quickly lost confidence in itself as a way to absolute truth, giving rise to relativism and nihilism in the nineteenth century. The example of Socrates was forgotten, and with it awareness of the need to choose between Athens and Jerusalem.

Strauss chose Athens over Jerusalem. But as a proud Jew who respected his people's belief, he also appreciated what religion at its highest development could offer as a way of life, especially for ordinary, nonreflective people.* Judaism was not *l'infâme*. And he did not believe that the Jewish difference could be abolished by assimilation. He seemed to share Franz Rosenzweig's view that Judaism, unlike Christianity, could never reconcile itself to history because it saw the truths vouchsafed to it through revelation as transhistorical. Modern Jewish thinkers who tried to blur the distinction between Judaism and Christianity and reform the faith in order to make it compatible with modern sensibilities would fail, and not only because of Christian prejudice.

---

* "Judaism is not a misfortune but, let us say, a 'heroic delusion.'... No nobler dream was ever dreamt. It is surely nobler to be a victim of the most noble dream than to profit from a sordid reality and to wallow in it.... The truth of the ultimate mystery—the truth that there is an ultimate mystery, that being is radically mysterious—cannot be denied even by the unbelieving Jew of our age." See "Why We Remain Jews" (1962), in *Jewish Philosophy and the Crisis of Modernity*, a collection of Strauss's writings on Judaism (SUNY Press, 1997).

The existence of the Jews will always remain a challenge to the Enlightenment's hope that politics can be isolated from claims about what lies beyond politics and be rationalized. The call of revelation cannot be extinguished from Jewish life, and therefore from politics; wherever there are Jews, there will be Jerusalem.

Strauss and Heidegger shared one large assumption: that the problems in Western civilization could be traced to the abandonment of a healthier, ur-mode of thought from the past. And Strauss, like Heidegger, spent much of his career trying to establish the decisive point when the great deviation took place. His seemingly scattered studies of past thinkers, which range masterfully if sometimes idiosyncratically across the classical Greek philosophers and dramatists, medieval Jewish and Muslim thinkers, and many of the major modern philosophers, are really exercises in philosophy looking for its lost original home. Of course, any such nostalgic quest already presumes the existence of what it then claims to discover: El Dorado. Strauss believed he found it in the works of Plato—but a Plato who needed to be freed from his modern interpreters.

The tradition that Strauss said he wanted to recover was, in his words, "zetetic" and "esoteric." *Zetesis* is a Greek term meaning inquiry or question, and is associated with *skepsis*, which has a similar meaning. Strauss understood Socrates to have been a zetetic thinker who only unraveled problems and left them in suspension, which differs from standard scholarly views of Socrates, especially in Plato's late works, as promoting elaborate doctrines regarding cosmology, epistemology, politics, and the soul. But Strauss went further to suggest that the ancient and medieval Platonic tradition that grew out of Socrates' activity practiced esotericism in political and pedagogical relations. This claim arose from his study of al-Farabi, the early medieval Islamic philosopher who also had a decisive influence on Maimonides, his medieval Jewish counterpart. The standard view of al-Farabi and of Maimonides is that they wanted to reconcile classical philosophy with revealed law. Strauss became convinced that this was an exoteric, publicly acceptable façade, and that behind it lay a subtler esoteric teaching.

As Strauss characterized them, al-Farabi and Maimonides were philosophers who found themselves faced with powerful conventions sanctioned by revealed religions unknown to the classical world. They saw that revelation and philosophy could never refute each other or be intellectually synthesized without abandoning one or the other. But they also understood that philosophy's skepticism could pose serious risks, whether to the philosopher himself or to the moral-legal foundation of the city, which rests at some level on unquestioned beliefs. Philosophy lives with a permanently open horizon, leaving unsettled many basic questions regarding morality and mortality. Most people, and all societies, need settled answers to those questions. So how is the philosopher to behave responsibly in such a situation, while still remaining himself?

According to Strauss, al-Farabi and Maimonides wrote in such a way that the casual reader would take away the lesson that philosophy and revelation are compatible. This exoteric lesson is doubly beneficial. It permits the philosopher to live and teach free of suspicion from theological and political authorities; it also plants the idea that those authorities must justify themselves before the tribunal of reason, thereby acting as a brake on superstition and tyranny. The attentive reader, however, will note that these texts are full of contradictions, lacunae, strange digressions, senseless repetitions, and silences. As the reader goes more deeply into them he begins to learn a different, esoteric lesson, which is that philosophy and revelation are not at all compatible. This esoteric lesson is also doubly beneficial. It teaches the reader that genuine philosophy can and should be kept free from all theological and political commitments; it also teaches him by example how to deal safely with conventional authority. The achievement of al-Farabi and Maimonides was to have demonstrated how philosophy can be both free when practiced esoterically and politically responsible when practiced exoterically.

After making this discovery Strauss then worked back in time, developing an idealized picture of an "ancient" or "classical" philosophical tradition that was also esoteric. He became fixed on establishing how this tradition disappeared in the modern era, turning the story into a *mythos* of the decline and fall of Western thought. (And by implication of

Western civilization.) Here Strauss's debt to Heidegger is most apparent. But reading them together also offers a lesson on the different ways that historical pessimism can translate itself into intellectual nostalgia, and then feed back into political action. Heidegger traveled this circuit himself, beginning as the great young hope of modern philosophy before becoming, a decade later, an enthusiastic fascist praising the "inner truth and greatness of National Socialism" and ending his life in political disgrace, all the while prophesying that "only a God can save us now." It is a very German story. Strauss passed a quiet, modest life teaching American students and writing his scholarly books, never engaging in politics. But in the decades following his death in 1973 a surprising number of those trained in the school he created have made careers not as philosophy professors but as engaged partisans in the politics of Washington. Theirs is a very American story.

Strauss came to America in the middle of his life, at the age of thirty-eight. He had spent most of the 1920s as an itinerant German scholar, working and teaching at various Jewish research centers while writing books on Spinoza and Maimonides. His circumstances finally changed in 1932 when he received a Rockefeller grant to do research in Paris, where he remained until 1934, and then in England, where he lived until 1937. In view of what was unfolding in Germany, the grant may have saved his life. Strauss published a much-admired book on Hobbes while in England, a country he loved, and, to judge by his correspondence, where he would have preferred to remain. But he had no academic prospects there, or in Palestine, where his friend Gershom Scholem failed to secure him a position.

In the end, Strauss looked to America, a country he had expressed no interest in until then. After spending a short time as a research fellow at Columbia University he obtained his first fixed teaching post at the New School for Social Research in 1938, where he spent ten obscure but intellectually productive years. In 1949 Strauss left the New School for the University of Chicago, where he would remain for the next two decades building the school that became "the Straussians."

Strauss went to Chicago at an important moment in the history of American higher education. World War II had just ended, Nazism had been defeated, and the cold war with Soviet communism had begun. The universities were expanding, both in size and in reach, and were admitting people who had previously been excluded. In such a setting one can imagine students' excitement when a short, unassuming foreigner with a high-pitched voice entered the classroom and began analyzing the great books, line by line, claiming that they treated the most urgent existential and political questions—and that they might contain the truth. The effect would have been intensified for Jewish-American students, who at a time when cultural assimilation still seemed the wisest course found themselves before a teacher who treated Judaism and the philosophical tradition with equal seriousness and dignity.

Strauss's pedagogical method was famous for its simplicity and directness. A student would be asked to read a passage from the work being discussed; Strauss would make a comment or two, noting contradictions or discrepancies with earlier passages; a student might then raise a question, which would lead Strauss to digress, taking it to a much higher level and illustrating it with often earthy examples. (He was particularly fond of examples from a newspaper advice column of the time, "Dear Abby.") Then on to the next passage. And that was all. No attempt was made to force the work into an arbitrary historical context; nor were there appeals to disembodied streams of thought. The only relevant questions were: What did Aristotle, or Maimonides, or Locke, or Nietzsche mean in this work? And, on a generous reading, could he possibly be right?*

Strauss's seminars were almost always devoted to single philosophical works, not to large swaths of intellectual history. But shortly after arriving at Chicago he was asked to deliver the prestigious Walgreen Lectures, which were finally published in 1953 as *Natural Right and History*. This work, his

---

*Thanks to the work of the Leo Strauss Center at the University of Chicago, many audio tapes and transcripts of Strauss's courses can now be consulted online. See leostrausscenter.uchicago.edu.

most influential, must be considered the founding document of the Straussian school. It was, so to speak, Strauss's application for citizenship and his way of accepting his academic chair in political science.

In the book he developed a number of original theses about the history of political philosophy, all directed against standard Whiggish accounts that described a steady rise from classical, to medieval Christian, to early-modern authoritarian, to late-modern democratic and socialist thought. Strauss claimed that, properly viewed, there had been a single coherent tradition of "classical natural right" running from Socrates to Thomas Aquinas. This tradition made a strict distinction between nature and convention, and argued that justice is what accords with the former, not the latter. Whether the rules of nature are discovered through philosophy or revelation, whether one account of nature is more persuasive than another, all this is less important, according to Strauss, than the conviction that natural justice is indeed the standard by which political arrangements must be judged. What Machiavelli represented, in Strauss's view, was a great rebellion against this standard—not only against Christianity but against the tradition of classical natural right as a whole. Once that break was made it was only a matter of time before modern thought—after making intermediate stops at liberalism and romanticism—descended into relativism and nihilism.

The dense and brilliant argument of *Natural Right and History* is put forward with unusual panache yet without sacrificing Strauss's characteristic directness and irony. Although it recounts a history of philosophy, it does so in a way that forces the reader to think hard about fundamental questions. Whether it convinces is another matter. Critics have charged Strauss with ignoring the very different historical periods in which his authors wrote, with underappreciating if not ignoring Christianity's break with the classical past and the Christian roots of early-modern discussions of human rights and limited government, and with many other errors. And even Strauss's students admit that his treatment of natural right is difficult to square with his treatment of the Socratic method, which involves questioning all appeals to authority, including that of nature.

But the real problems with *Natural Right and History* were not historical, they were pedagogical. Had Strauss returned to continental Europe to teach after the war, his students already would have studied the history of philosophy, however superficially, in high school. That might have made them more susceptible to historicism and relativism, and hostile to the very idea of natural right. But in return they probably would have been more inclined—as are his European admirers today—to see Strauss himself as a thinker exploring the philosophical tradition for his own purposes. His American followers have had difficulty seeing him in that light, as an original thinker whose example might help them to follow their own paths in thinking. They treat him less like Socrates than like Moses, and *Natural Right and History* as tablets brought down from the mountain. In a little more than three hundred pages, the book offered American students unfamiliar with any other account of philosophy's history an epic, just-so version of it, tracing our intellectual decline from the Golden Age of Athens to the modern Age of Iron. It is a script. But unlike the script one might be taught in a European high school, along with others, this script gave the United States an important place in the unfolding of a single story.

Strauss introduced the book with the words of the Declaration of Independence, "we hold these truths to be self-evident," and then asked: Do we still? Does the contemporary West still believe in natural "inalienable Rights," or do we rather believe, as Strauss dryly puts it, that "all men are endowed by the evolutionary process or by a mysterious fate with many kinds of urges and aspirations, but certainly with no natural right"? If the latter, doesn't that mean that modern liberalism has declined into relativism, and isn't that indistinguishable from the kind of nihilism that gave rise to the political disasters of the twentieth century? "The contemporary rejection of natural right leads to nihilism," Strauss writes, "nay, it is identical with nihilism." As a rhetorical device for piquing interest in the apparently antiquarian task of recovering classical philosophy, this introduction succeeds brilliantly. But it also raises the peculiar thought that such an enterprise is wrapped up with American destiny.

Strauss never wrote a single essay about American thought and only a few shorter pieces on "the crisis of our time," forgettable exercises in Weimar *Kulturpessimismus* that display little feel for American life. After *Natural Right and History* he spent most of his time at Chicago teaching courses on important European figures in the history of philosophy, concentrating mainly on their political works. His students then were also, like him, mainly interested in studying old books, in reviving *la querelle des anciens et des modernes*, and adapting an aristocratic understanding of the philosophical life to the slightly vulgar American democratic setting. They did their best to imitate Strauss, the main difference being the missionary zeal and rhetoric of moral uplift that sometimes suffused their writings. A few of Strauss's early students got involved with contemporary politics (one wrote speeches for the 1964 Republican presidential candidate, Barry Goldwater) and it is true that conservatives were drawn to him because of his skepticism toward modern ideas of progress and his hostility to communism. But so were cold war liberals who shared his admiration for Lincoln and wanted to have a clear understanding of liberal democracy's weaknesses in order to protect it. Most were probably Democrats in those years and supported the civil rights movement, but the Straussian school remained scholarly, not partisan.

After 1968, all that changed. The universities imploded, and the Straussians took the student revolts, and all that followed in American society, particularly hard. From Strauss they had learned to see genuine education as a necessarily elite enterprise that is difficult to maintain in a leveling, democratic society. And thanks to *Natural Right and History*, they were also prepared to see the threat of "nihilism" lurking in the interstices of modern life, waiting to be released and to turn America into Weimar. This was the premise underlying Allan Bloom's best seller *The Closing of the American Mind* (1987), and helps to explain why its genuine insights into American youth got buried in *Weltschmertz* and doomsaying. Bloom and several other influential Straussians spent the 1960s at Cornell University, which had a particularly ugly experience with student violence, race-baiting, and liberal cowardice in the face of attacks on the university. Buildings were seized, faculty were threatened, the university's president assaulted. That moment seems to have been an apocalyptic revelation for Bloom, opening his eyes to the fact that "whether it be Nuremberg or Woodstock, the principle is the same" and that "Enlightenment in America came close to breathing its last during the sixties."

After the 1960s, one began to see a new, more political catechism developing among certain of Strauss's disciples. There are still plenty of Straussians who are nonpartisan and only devote themselves to teaching old books. But many others, traumatized by the changes in American universities and society, began gravitating toward the circles of neoconservatives then forming in New York and Washington. The catechism these political Straussians began to teach their students is nowhere recorded, and not because there is a secret doctrine being passed around by esoteric means. The catechism so permeates the way they think about Strauss today, and therefore about themselves and their country, that its philosophical and political tenets need not be articulated.

It begins with the assumption that the modern liberal West is in crisis, unable to defend itself intellectually against internal and external enemies, who are abetted by historical relativism. This crisis obliges us to understand how modern thought reached such an impasse, which takes us back to the break with classical thought. There we discover the prudence of classical philosophy, which trained its adepts directly, and statesmen indirectly, about natural right and the fundamental problems of politics. This practice, it is then suggested, deserves to be recovered, especially in the United States, which was founded self-consciously on the idea of natural right and therefore still takes it seriously. Such an exercise would not only shore up the American polity, it would contribute to the defense of liberal democracy everywhere. The unspoken conclusion: America has a redemptive historical mission—an idea nowhere articulated by Strauss himself.

The year 2003 marked the thirtieth anniversary of Strauss's death. In that year several superb studies of his thought were published in Europe, where his posthumous reputation keeps growing and translations of his writings keep appearing. An edition of his collected works, edited by a German scholar, proceeds apace and has piqued interest in Strauss's early engagement with Zionism, his views about Judaism, his critique of the Enlightenment, and the "theological-political problem" more generally. The edition also helps to place him more centrally in the German Jewish culture of Weimar and reveals him to be one of the great minds of his generation. His European readers have no interest in and little knowledge of the political engagements of his American disciples.

But this was not the Strauss discussed and rumored about in the United States in 2003. The anniversary of his death happened to coincide with the American invasion of Iraq, and in the lead-up to the war, journalists began noticing that several of its prominent advocates had studied in the Straussian school. The idea began circulating that Strauss himself was the master thinker behind the interventionist policy of democracy promotion developed by American neoconservatives. Writers who had never read him trawled his dense commentaries on ancient, medieval, and modern political thought looking for incriminating evidence. Finding none, some suggested that Strauss never wrote what he thought, that his secret political doctrines were passed on esoterically to adepts who subsequently infiltrated American government and operated duplicitously. At the ideological fringes the term "cabal" was occasionally employed, in ignorance (one hopes) of its anti-Semitic connotations.

The suspicions regarding Leo Strauss and the Iraq War were misplaced and the whole affair was unseemly. But the connection between the Straussians and the American right is quite real. From reading Strauss his disciples learn that although philosophers should not try to realize ideal cities, they do bear responsibility for the cities in which they find themselves. From their teachers they then learn about the importance of defending liberal democracy against the threats it faces, at home and abroad. After that they are fed a lot of cloying scholarship about the American founding, the glories of statesmanship, the burden of prudence, and the need for civic virtue. They are also encouraged to think that America has been slipping into nihilism since the 1960s and that, however vulgar, right-wing populism and religious fundamentalism contribute to the nation's recovering its basic sense of right and wrong. This is the path that led from the seminar rooms in Chicago to the right-wing political-media-foundation complex in Washington that has transformed American politics over the past five decades. It is a long way from Athens.

The ironies in this short chapter of American intellectual history are almost too many to number. Where but in America could a European thinker convinced of the elite nature of genuine education produce pupils who would go on to make common cause with populist politicians? Where but in America could a teacher of esotericism, concerned about protecting philosophical inquiry from political harm, find his books used to train young people to become guardians of an ephemeral ideology? Where but in America could the Socratic practice of skeptical questioning inspire professions of faith in a national ideal? Yes, Henry James was right: America is hard on all European legacies.

Currents

FROM LUTHER TO WALMART

The possession of ancestral furniture changes its
meaning in an antiquarian soul: for the soul is
rather possessed by the furniture.

—Nietzsche

People who live in a golden age usually go around
complaining how yellow everything looks.

—Randall Jarrell

THERE ARE ONLY so many ways of recounting a history. The
oldest and most enduring is the chronicle. Chronicles all look
something like the Bayeux Tapestry, the eleventh-century
embroidered scroll that visualizes the stream of events leading up to the Norman Conquest. As the scroll unfurls you
see men fighting on ships, followed by men fighting on horse-
back, followed by men fighting with swords, with the occa-
sional lord and castle thrown in for variety. This goes on for
more than two hundred feet. Since chronicles try to be

comprehensive, they are wonderfully messy documents—
messy like reality. They leave the impression that the outcomes of human action depend on choices the actors make in
time, that they are weaving the tapestry as they go.

The Hebrew Bible belongs in this tradition. What makes
the chronicle of the covenant so dramatic is that it follows
the unpredictable encounter of divine and human freedom in
all its emotional twists and turns. God chose Abraham, but
would Abraham choose God? In the event, he did; but then
Isaac had to choose whether to remain faithful to their covenant, as did Jacob and Esau, and so on down the line. The
story that emerges is meaningful not because it exposes the
irresistible work of providence, but because it doesn't. It
teaches that you must choose to be chosen.

Human beings should be content with such stories and
the gods who come with them. But few of us are. Chronicles
place the responsibility for history on our very small shoulders, which is a burden we would gladly shirk. We want
comfort. So from time immemorial we have fabricated myths
to convince ourselves that we understand the underlying
processes by which the world took on its present shape. Such
myths begin with some remote historical Big Bang, after
which life unfolds in a meaningful, if not precisely predictable, direction. It is a revealing psychological fact that the
most common historical myths with which early civilizations
comforted themselves were stories of fated decline, which
give temporal reasons for why life is so hard. We suffer because we live in the Age of Iron, far removed from our origins

in the Age of Gold. If we are good perhaps one day the gods will smile down and return us to the world we have lost.

Christianity turned its back on these ancient stories of fated decline. But it has never been able to escape historical mythmaking, despite the best efforts of theologians from Augustine to Karl Barth. The reason, as Hegel formulated it so well, is that Christian revelation is based on a unique divine incursion into the flow of historical time that altered but did not delegitimize an earlier divine–human relationship. Christianity therefore begs for a story that connects the historical periods created by this event: the age before the Incarnation, the age of the present saeculum, and the age to be inaugurated by Christ's redemptive return. Eusebius of Caesarea, in the early fourth century CE, was the first Christian thinker to have a serious go at this, and his progressive narrative shaped much subsequent Western thinking about history. In his account, God used one providential hand to "prepare the Gospel" by guiding Hebrew history from Abraham to Jesus; with the other hand, He built Rome up from a small republic to a vast and powerful empire. With the conversion of Constantine to Christianity these two trajectories met, fusing divine truth with mundane power and inaugurating a new epoch of God's kingdom on earth. Against the pessimistic pagan myth of the World We Have Lost, Eusebius offered his optimistic Goodbye to All That.

Eusebianism is a theological trap, though. For from the moment bad things start to happen, the myth, and the hopes attached to it, begin to crumble. Augustine saw this firsthand after the sack of Rome in 410. Despair was immediate and widespread among Roman Christians, who began to wonder whether they were being punished by the ancient pagan gods they had abandoned. To shore them up Augustine wrote the *City of God*, which still stands as the greatest Christian work on history ever written. Augustine did more than refute his pagan adversaries, who blamed the Roman collapse on the effeminate corruptions of Christianity. He reoriented Christian thinking away from the flow of history and toward its eschatological end. We do not know why God allowed pagan Rome to flourish and then joined it with the Church, Augustine tells his readers. Nor do we know why He allowed it to collapse. That's God's business. Ours is to preach the Gospel, be righteous, remain faithful, and serve Him. The rest is in His hands.

Though the *City of God* became a foundation stone of Catholic theology almost from the moment it appeared, the temptation of Eusebianism remained great—even for Augustine himself, who while writing his masterwork asked his disciple Orosius to write a *History Against the Pagans*, which demonstrated how life had in fact progressively improved since the advent of Christianity, just in case that argument, too, was needed. This tension—between Augustine's image of the pilgrim Church just passing through and Eusebius's image of the Church triumphant—was never resolved in the Catholic Middle Ages. And for a good reason: despite centuries of internal conflicts over papal authority and external conflicts with the Eastern Church and the Turks, the Roman Catholic Church did indeed seem triumphant.

Until the Protestant Reformation. The shock of the Reformation for medieval Christians was as great as that experienced by Roman Christians after 410, with one important difference: after the assaults of Luther, Calvin, and the radical reformers, the Roman Catholic Church never got its modern Augustine. Not after the Enlightenment, either—or the American and French Revolutions, or the industrial revolution, or the socialist revolutions of the nineteenth century, or the spread of Darwinism, or the secularization of European schools, or the extension of the suffrage, or the rise of communism and fascism, or decolonization, or birth control, or feminism, or any other major historical change in the modern era. The Church responded to most of these challenges in its traditional way: first condemning the innovators, then tolerating some differences, and finally declaring that such innovations had been continuous with Catholic doctrine all along. But the Church is slow and modern history moves fast. Which is why, in the five centuries since the Protestant Reformation, it has never found its historical equipoise. The Church has no widely accepted theology of history to speak of, just a stream of papal encyclicals that reflect the shifting moods of this or that pontiff. *Thinking* modern history has largely been left to lay intellectuals.

The golden age of lay Catholic historiography was the nineteenth century, when counterrevolutionary thinkers such as Bonald, the young Lamennais, Maistre, and Donoso Cortés refined the World We Have Lost narrative that has nour-ished reactionary political movements ever since. But in the twentieth century lay and clerical writers developed a kinder, gentler variation of it that has not lost its appeal among Catholics. Let's call it the Road Not Taken.

Those who recount this kind of story tell us that at some point in medieval or early-modern history the West took a momentous wrong turn, putting itself on the path to our modernity with all its attendant problems. But no single per-son or event was responsible for this. The blame must be shared by philosophers, theologians, and the Church hierar-chy itself. This was a tragic development: had everyone only been more patient, the Church would have continued evolv-ing, and in a good direction. The Middle Ages would eventu-ally have waned and a new society would have developed. But the swings of modern history would have been less ex-treme and the worst avoided. Change would have been more gradual, radical attacks on the Church would have been un-necessary, and the Church in turn would not have fallen into the reactionary crouch it maintained from the French Revo-lution until Vatican II. With moral debate confined within the flexible bounds of Catholic orthodoxy, important human values would have been preserved from secular dogmatism and skepticism. We would have been spared the brutality of the industrial era, the monsters of modern science, and the empty individualism of our time. All in all, we would be liv-ing a happier, more fruitful and humane existence.

Some stimulating Catholic works have been written in

this genre. Among the best is *Reason and Revelation in the Middle Ages*, by the great French medievalist Étienne Gilson. Based on a series of lectures that Gilson gave in 1937 at the University of Virginia, it traces the history of Catholic theology from its anti-intellectual origins in Church Fathers such as Tertullian to the hyperrationalism of late scholasticism, both of which Gilson rejected. He adopted the classic Thomist position that Aquinas and only Aquinas managed to reconcile reason and revelation in a way that did justice to the truths of theology and philosophy. But once the grand Thomist synthesis was undermined by Ockhamists, Scotists, and other schoolmen hoping to improve on it, reaction set in, preparing the way for Martin Luther's crude *sola scriptura* and Descartes's cold scientific rationalism. Both have been disasters for the Western mind. Yet the *Summa Theologiae* is still there, beckoning on the Road Not Taken.

Other works in this style have been more political. During World War II two forceful intellectual histories were published by European Jesuits, one in Switzerland, the other in occupied France. Hans Urs von Balthasar's monumental and hugely influential *Apocalypse of the German Soul* traced the Promethean streak in modern German thought from the Idealists and Romantics down to Heidegger and Karl Barth. Henri de Lubac's *The Drama of Atheist Humanism* portrayed nineteenth-century thinkers such as Comte, Marx, and Nietzsche as prophets of modern man's self-deification, which led inexorably to man's dehumanization. Urs von Balthasar and Lubac were not simple declinists, though, and they did not romanticize an imaginary lost world. They told their stories to turn attention back to an abandoned intellectual tradition they hoped to revive after the catastrophe of world war.

Most of us today do not believe that we live in such catastrophic times. But over the past thirty years the Road Not Taken genre has come back into vogue among a new generation of antimodern Catholics (and some Anglicans) on the left and the right, from members of the postmodern Radical Orthodoxy movement in Britain to American theoconservatives. And they have all taken their cue from what has turned out to be one of the most influential books of our time: Alasdair MacIntyre's *After Virtue*, which appeared in 1981. By blurring the lines between intellectual history and philosophical argument, MacIntyre—a former Marxist who converted to Catholicism—developed a compelling just-so story about how our dark world came to be. Once upon a time the Aristotelian tradition of moral reflection, which ran continuously from antiquity through the Catholic Middle Ages, gave Europeans a coherent narrative for understanding and practicing virtue in their individual and collective lives. That tradition was destroyed by the "Enlightenment project," which undid the work of centuries—not only the work of the Church, but the work any healthy society undertakes to ground morality in a living tradition of practice. By destroying this tradition the Enlightenment unwittingly prepared the way for acquisitive capitalism, Nietzscheanism, and the relativistic liberal emotivism we live with today, in a society that "cannot hope to achieve moral consensus." MacIntyre expressed no explicit hope or desire to return to the Middle Ages. Instead, his book ends with a visionary call for creating new moral communities based on old modes of thought, where a coherent moral life might once again be sustained. The final sentence reads: "We are waiting not for a Godot, but for another—doubtless very different—St. Benedict."

After Virtue is not an academic work of history and does not pretend to be. It is a strong work of advocacy that ends with a kind of prayer. The same is true of historian Brad Gregory's *The Unintended Reformation*, an enormous and widely discussed work inspired by MacIntyre's example.* At first glance it appears to be a conventional history, with ambitious chapters on post-Reformation developments in philosophy, politics, education, economics, and civil society, supplemented by 150 pages of rich footnotes. But the deeper you delve into this book, the more you begin to feel that you are watching a shadow-puppet play on the wall of some Vatican cave. A straightforward history of the post-Reformation West written from an explicitly Catholic standpoint would have been a welcome addition to our understanding of the period and of ourselves. Instead, Gregory has offered up a sly crypto-Catholic travel brochure for the Road Not Taken that has been warmly received by critics of contemporary

---

The Unintended Reformation: How a Religious Revolution Secularized Society (Harvard University Press, 2012).

liberal society on the right and the left. The craving for theological-political mythmaking has somehow survived the ravages of our secular age.

The book's aim, he tells us, is to explain "how Europe and North America today came to be as they are." (After the book's second page contemporary Europe is hardly mentioned, making this yet another US-centric history of "the West.") And how do we live now? Not well. Gregory worries that our political life is polarized, that "Walmart capitalism and consumerism" are idealized, that environmental degradation is accelerating at an alarming rate, that standards in schools are declining, and that public discourse is governed by ideological correctness and cultural relativism. For Gregory these vast and various problems have a single source: the "hyper-pluralism" of modern societies. This term appears with metronomic regularity here, modified by a torrent of adjectives like "never-ending," "confusing," "unintended," "unwelcome," "gangrenous," and "hegemonic." "All Westerners," Gregory declares at one point, "live in the Kingdom of Whatever."

Except when they don't. For by now this hyper-pluralism has been so deeply rooted in our institutions, especially universities, that those who question it are excommunicated from intellectual life. On the one hand, "within the limits of the law, literally anything goes as far as truth claims and religious practices are concerned"; on the other, "the religious truth claims made by billions of people are excluded from consideration on their own terms in nearly all research universities," where "those who reject any substantive religious answers to the Life Questions ... are statistically over-represented." What bothers him is not that there is no social consensus but that the one we have supports moral pluralism. "There is no shared, substantive common good, nor are there any realistic prospects for devising one (at least in the immediately foreseeable future)." Nor can we expect help from Catholic universities, which in their rush to appear accepting of modernity have "unwittingly invited in an intellectual Trojan horse bearing a load of subversive assumptions."

Gregory tells two unconnected stories about how everything went wrong, hoping perhaps that if one doesn't persuade his reader the other will. The first is about the historical Reformation. Gregory does not provide even a brief history of the Catholic Middle Ages that preceded the Reformation, only a single, static, rose-tinted image of the World We Have Lost. (He also avoids the term "Catholic," preferring instead "medieval Christianity," which sounds more inclusive.) If not an entirely happy world, it was at least a relatively harmonious one, despite what everyone thinks. Yes, there were theological disagreements and conflicts over authority, pitting popes against monastic orders against Church councils against emperors against princes. Yes, the Church split into East and West, and for a time there were rival popes. And yes, mistakes were made. Heretics were roughly handled, pointless Crusades launched, Jews and Muslims expelled or worse. Still, through it all, the Catholic *complexio oppositorum* was held together by a unified institutionalized view of the human good. "Over the course of more than a millennium the church had gradually and unsystematically institutionalized throughout Latin Europe a comprehensive sacramental worldview based on truth claims about God's actions in history, centered on the incarnation, life, teachings, death, and resurrection of Jesus of Nazareth." And this translated into a "shared, social life of faith, hope, love, humility, patience, self-sacrifice, forgiveness, compassion, service, and generosity [that] simply was Christianity." He offers no evidence for this statement for the simple reason that none could possibly exist.

Then came the catastrophe. The Church itself was largely to blame for creating the conditions that the early Reformers complained of, and for not policing itself. The charges leveled by Luther and Calvin had merit, and theirs was originally a conservative rebellion aimed at returning the Church to its right mind. But then things got out of hand, as the intoxicating spirit of rebellion spread to the spiritual Jacobins of the radical Reformation. They are our real founding fathers and bequeathed to us not a coherent set of moral and theological doctrines but the corrosive pluralism that characterizes our age. The radicals denied the need for sacraments or relics, which ordinary believers believed in, handing them Bibles they were unequipped to understand. *Sola scriptura*, plus the idea that anyone could be filled with the Holy Spirit, inspired every radical reformer to become his own Saint Paul—and then demand that his neighbors put down their nets and follow him. Disagreements erupted, leading to war, which led to the creation of confessional states, which led to more wars. Modern liberalism was born to cope with these conflicts, which it did. But the price was high: it required the institutionalization of toleration as the highest moral virtue. The nineteenth-century Catholic Church rejected this whole package and withdrew within its walls, where intellectual life declined and dogma ossified. It thus left the rest of us to sink ever deeper into the confusing, unsatisfying, hyper-pluralistic, consumer-driven, dogmatically relativistic world of today.

And that's how we got from Luther to Walmart.

If this story doesn't convince you, though, Gregory has another. This one, which has little to do with the Reformation, focuses on transformations in medieval theology and early modern philosophy that prepared what he takes to be our contemporary outlook. At the heart of the matter is the old quarrel between affirmative theology and negative theology—very roughly, over whether we can speak meaningfully of the attributes of God, or whether He is the He of whom nothing can be said. Gregory believes that how one thinks about this question can affect how one thinks about nearly everything else. But even if you share his view (I do), it does not follow that theological disputes of this kind actually *did* change the way people at every level of Christian society thought about the human condition. This slippage is typical of mytho-histories.

Gregory is committed to the view that before the Reformation the harmony of the heavens was mirrored in Christian life and thought. This leads him to assert (argue would be too strong a word) that before the late-medieval writings of Duns Scotus and William of Ockham, something called "traditional Christian metaphysics" held sway and leaned in a somewhat negative theological direction. According to "traditional Christian teaching," he writes, "God is literally unimaginable and incomprehensible." It is hard to know what he means by "traditional" here, given the centuries of disagreement about just what it means to say that God is, or acts providentially, or performs miracles, or was incarnated, or can be understood, or is present in the Holy Eucharist. (It was because medieval Christian thought was so pluralistic that Thomas Aquinas felt compelled to make order out of chaos in his *Summa Theologiae*.) Or to know how such a metaphysics manifested itself at the popular level, where ordinary clergy and common believers thought of God as the Big Bearded Being, took miracles to be the direct work of His hands, venerated the saints and their sacred relics, practiced magic, and swallowed the host whole, lest their teeth add wounds to the flesh of Christ.

Modern Thomists have long asserted that the departures from the *Summa* by Scotus and then Ockham unintentionally paved the way for modern philosophy and science. The (simplified) argument is this: Scotus compromised God's transcendence by claiming that a single concept of being applies both to Him and to His creation, whereas Thomas had said that only an analogy could be established between them. Once God and creation were thought to inhabit the same mountain, so to speak, the question arose how far up the slope one needed to go to explain things farther down. The answer of modern science would be: not very far. God is a hypothesis that we can, for practical purposes, do without. For Thomists such as Gilson, the decoupling of modern science from theology, and subsequently from morality, was foreordained by these two subtle theological departures from the grand *Summa*.

Gregory, though, is not interested in defending Thomism— or even theology, which he appears to distrust, believing perhaps that it is incapable of proving what he wants it to prove. So like many American theoconservatives, he makes a populist turn. He is annoyed not only that "religion is not and cannot be considered a potential source of knowledge," just "a matter of subjective opinion and personal preference," but also by the contemporary secular assumption that "knowledge must be based on evidence, it must make sense" and that it "must be universal and objective: if something is known or knowable, its content is not contingent on who discovers it." He wants to defend other "ways" of knowing, which he calls "salvific participatory" and "experiential," along with "a sacramental view of reality."

At this point a narcotic haze descends on the book. Gregory wants us to believe that medieval Christendom before the theological fall seamlessly harmonized distinct "kinds" of knowledge, blending theology, natural science, and "individually differentiated participatory knowledge of the faith and its shared way of life, based ultimately and above all on God's actions in Jesus." And what was the nature and content of that knowledge, exactly? Gregory never explains. Perhaps by its very nature it cannot be communicated verbally. The most we are told about Christian life in the old days is that "the better that one lived it—the holier one was—the clearer did [God's] truth become, a *sapientia* beyond mere *scientia*. The lived holy wisdom of the saints, quite apart from whether they were erudite or brilliant, embodied most conspicuously this sort of knowledge." If that claim is obscure, the following one is not: in medieval Christianity, "the pursuit of knowledge for some other end, or as an end in itself, was literally vain in the sense of purposeless."

Faith seeking understanding, with a curfew at eleven— that is Gregory's historical, and apparently future, ideal. What happened to it? Late scholasticism, which pursued its dialectical games late into the night, mindless of the lived faith of others, shares part of the blame. Then, of course, the Bible was "let loose among the 'common man'" by the Reformation. After that, states and universities became divided by confession, knowledge became a tool of state power, scripture was subjected to the higher criticism, and disciplines became separated from each other. In Europe, Wilhelm von Humboldt's modern research university distanced itself from religious questions and affiliations, and in the United States religious colleges governed by milquetoast liberal Protestants eventually succumbed to this German virus, giving birth to our centerless multiversity, which spawned today's antirational, anything-goes postmodernism.

And that's how we got from scholasticism to structuralism.

It's quite a story, or two stories, that Gregory tells. Now let's consider a third.

Once upon a time, when men were heroes and Jupiter was venerated, a provincial prophet declared himself to be the Son of God and developed a following among anticolonial zealots, mystical cave dwellers, resentful slaves, and housewives on the Roman Palatine. Their antinomian movement brought chaos to a flexible, complex pagan world and upset its settled moral understanding of life. There followed a contest for command among rival Judeo-Christian and gnostic sectarians armed with different scriptures, in a war of words that soon involved Monarchians, Montanists, Arians, Nestorians, Pelagians, and countless other soon-to-be-declared heretics. As they argued about absurd matters such as whether spirit can be made flesh, partisans of the old gods shook their heads, pointed to the corruptions of their virtuous *Romanitas*, and blamed everything on the warring upstarts.

After a few centuries, though, things settled down. Antinomianism gave way to a loose theological-political orthodoxy that blessed a new civilization with a coherent moral order, new stocks of learning, and extraordinary artistic achievements. It lasted a millennium. But then a second biblically inspired movement, also appealing to the disadvantaged, came along and undid the work of centuries. Another contest for command arose among radical sectarians divided over absurdities; all coherence was lost. And once again, after five centuries, things settled down, and today there is a new moral-political orthodoxy we can call individualism. Though it lacks theological trappings, it actually owes a great deal to Jesus, who was a libertarian *avant la lettre* prophesying the final triumph of the individual soul and its inner experience over the domination of traditional communal bonds and illegitimate religious authority. The new orthodoxy brought a perfectly coherent worldview that makes sense of the human condition (we are bodies that are born and die alone), of what lies beyond (nothing), and of what we need to be happy (carpe diem). And it also, not insignificantly, keeps the peace, since war is bad for business. The new catechism has not reached everyone, and resistance in certain regions is strong and sometimes armed. But if these retrogrades do not convert, their children or grandchildren eventually will. And the world will be as one.

It's a compelling story—and an old one, pieced together with fragments from Julian the Apostate, Eusebius, Otto of Freising, Bacon, Condorcet, Hegel, Feuerbach, and today's Silicon Valley futurists. Of course, it is nothing but a myth—not a lie, just an imaginative assemblage of past events and ideas and present hopes and fears. As is Brad Gregory's *The Unintended Reformation*.

Why do people still feel the need for such myths? For the same reason people always have. We want the comfort, however cold, of thinking that we understand the present, while at the same time escaping full responsibility for the future. There is a book to be done on Western mytho-histories in relation to the times in which they were written, and the social-psychological work they accomplished in different epochs. Such a book would trace how, beginning in the early nineteenth century, archaic theological narratives about the past were modernized and substituted for argument in intellectual proxy wars over the present. Gregory is obviously dissatisfied with the way we live now and despairs that things will only get worse—not an irrational worry. But what help is it to imagine that "medieval Christendom failed, the Reformation failed, confessionalized Europe failed, and Western modernity is failing," as if civilizations pass through discrete periods defined by a single "project"? Life does not work that way; history does not work that way. Nor does it help to imagine that the peak of Western civilization was reached in the decades just before the Reformation—any more than it helps Muslims to imagine that the peak of Islamic civilization was reached during the reign of the early caliphs, or in medieval Spain. Such myths do nothing but feed a more insidious dream: that political action might help us find our way back to the Road Not Taken. The lesson of Saint Augustine remains as timely as it was fifteen hundred years ago: that we are destined to pave our road as we go. And that the rest is in God's hands.

FROM MAO TO SAINT PAUL

*Not the least among the tasks now confronting
thought is that of placing all the reactionary arguments against Western culture in the service of
progressive enlightenment.*

—Theodor Adorno

THE EARLY CHURCH Father Tertullian called Saint Paul "the
apostle of the heretics" for good reason. Ever since Marcion,
the second-century theologian who appealed to Paul's authority for his doctrine that the Christian God was a deity
wholly distinct from and superior to the Hebrews' Yahweh,
the Pauline corpus has been creatively misread. It is hard to
find much in Jesus's Sermon on the Mount to inspire such
flights of fancy, but Paul's epistles, with their powerful intimations about sin, grace, and imminent redemption, are another matter. As Monsignor Ronald Knox put it in his classic
study *Enthusiasm*, "the mind of Paul has been misunderstood

all down the centuries; there is no aberration of Christianity which does not point to him as the source of its inspiration, found as a rule, in his Epistle to the Romans."

And one can understand why. Consider these extraordinarily pregnant formulations from the Epistle: "We hold that a person is justified by faith apart from works prescribed by the law" (3:28). Does this mean that pure interior faith trumps all law, whether Jewish, Roman, Greek—or modern? Or that works are without ultimate importance? "For there is no distinction between Jew and Greek; the same Lord is lord of all" (10:12). Does this mean the absolute universality of the new religious and moral precepts, abolishing all cultural particularity? "And those whom he predestined he also called; and those whom he called he also justified; and those whom he justified he also glorified. What then are we to say about these things? If God is for us, who is against us?" (8:30–31). Does this mean, following the previous verses, that those called by God are justified in tearing down the law and bringing the world universal truth even against resistance? These heretical interpretations may be philologically unsound, but what does philology matter when, as Paul himself put it, "creation waits with eager longing for the revealing of the children of God" (8:19)?

Throughout Christian history Saint Paul's importance waxed and waned. But he has never been out of favor with those aching to escape an unbearable present and bring about our future redemption. One need not even believe in

Christ's divinity to believe that His most radical disciple shows us the way to a better future.

If you wander into an American religious bookstore today you will find very few books on Paul's epistles, and fewer still worth reading. But if you stroll the aisles of a secular university bookstore you will discover a surprising number of works about him, not devotional but political. There is a lot of thought being given to Saint Paul these days by those intellectually committed to critical theory, deconstruction, postmodernism, postcolonial studies, and the like. How the students of "theory" became amateur Bible scholars is an instructive story. It involves the disappointments with Marxism in the 1960s, the turn to deconstruction and identity politics in the 1970s, and the flirtation with Walter Benjamin's messianic ideas in the 1980s. But it is the lingering enchantment with the former Nazi jurist Carl Schmitt and his notion of "political theology" that explains the Paul vogue on the European and American academic left.*

The first figure to promote Paul as a resource for the left was Jacob Taubes, a Jewish admirer of Schmitt's who died in 1987. A generation younger than Leo Strauss and Eric Voegelin, Taubes was born in Switzerland in 1923 into a distinguished rabbinic family and was himself ordained in the 1940s. After the war, and after publishing his one book, a

---

*See my *The Reckless Mind*, chapter 2.

study of Western eschatology, he became a peripatetic professor and political gadfly moving restlessly between New York, Berlin, Jerusalem, and Paris. Anyone who encountered him came away with a Taubes story. In New York you learn that in the late 1940s he taught Talmud to some future neoconservatives; in Jerusalem you learn that he was involved with heterodox Christian monks; and in Berlin you find a photo of him addressing a demonstration of 1960s radicals while Rudi Dutschke and Herbert Marcuse sit admiringly at his side. The Berlin years made Taubes's reputation. He was everything young Germans could possibly have wanted in a sage: an old left-wing Jew blessing their revolution, not with the stale scientific formulas of orthodox Marxism but with the biblical language of redemption. Taubes eventually soured on the radicals but he bequeathed to them a way of seeing politics through the crypto-religious lenses of Benjamin and Schmitt. A few months before his death he gave a set of informal lectures in Heidelberg on Saint Paul and Schmitt, which he intended as a kind of last intellectual testament. When the transcripts were published in Germany they found a large public, and by now translations have appeared in many European languages, including in English as *The Political Theology of Paul.*

Taubes made two large claims about Saint Paul. The first is that, far from betraying the Jews, he was a distinctively Jewish fanatic sent to universalize the Bible's hope of redemption, bringing this revolutionary new idea to the wider world. After Moses, there was never a better Jew than Paul.

"I regard him," says Taubes dryly, "as more Jewish than any Reform rabbi, or any Liberal rabbi, I ever heard in Germany, England, America, Switzerland, or anywhere." Mainstream Jews were baffled when Taubes declared himself to be a Pauline Jew; he would respond that while Jeremiah was a prophet from and to the Jews, Paul showed it is possible to be "an apostle *from the Jews* to the nations"—which is also how the immodest Taubes saw himself.

The second claim was the really important one: that "for Paul, the task at hand is the *establishment and legitimation of a new people of God*." This is an example of what Schmitt called "political theology," a term he gave a special meaning. Political theology, in his sense, concerns the way in which legal and political structures acquire or lose legitimacy, a process that he argued depended on an arbitrary decision made by a "sovereign," whether human or divine, and which revealed itself whenever those orders broke down in a "state of exception" (for example, when a constitution was suspended in an emergency). Every society, according to Schmitt, rests implicitly on a kind of political revelation from above that reflects no universal principle and recognizes no natural bound, just a will and capacity to make something be. Seen from a theological angle, God created a community devoted to Him by giving Moses the Ten Commandments; seen from a political angle, Moses was invoking God to legitimate his own act of state-creation. For Taubes as for Schmitt, all serious politics has this mysterious double character.

Taubes's reading of Paul's Epistle to the Romans offers a

good example of this theological-political thinking. Taubes homes in on Paul's antinomianism—his relentless attack on Jewish and Roman law as the enemies to be vanquished if the Bible's messianic promise was to reach the whole of mankind. Paul's declaration that "you are not under law but under grace" (Romans 6:14) announces a double coup d'état against Moses and Caesar, a sovereign decision establishing a new world order. Jesus has virtually no part in this reading of early Christianity; he was just a martyr in the early years of the insurgency. The real revolutionary was Paul, who imagined a utopian order and brought it about through theological-political fiat. "Compared to this," Taubes declared, "all the little revolutionaries are *nothing.*"

With the publication of Taubes's lectures in 1993 the Pauline moment on the European left had begun. Books and articles on Paul have been trickling out ever since, some interesting, most dreadful. And the most surprising was surely the one by Alain Badiou. A student of the Marxist theorist Louis Althusser in the early 1960s, a radical Maoist and defender of the Khmer Rouge in the 1970s, Badiou, now nearly eighty, still writes warmly about the Chinese Cultural Revolution. It came as a shock in France, then, when Badiou published *Saint Paul: The Foundation of Universalism* in 1997, calling on the left to rediscover the radical universalism of Saint Paul and apply it to revolutionary politics. He had become an inspired Pauline fanatic.

"For me," Badiou once told *Le Monde*, "May '68 was a fall on the road to Damascus." Whether he ever regained his sight can be debated. It is quite an experience to read through his political writings, most of which have now appeared in English. It is not every day that one finds a defense of Mao's personality cult, and in quasi-theological terms no less. In one essay Badiou calls Mao an "aesthetic genius," adding that "there are moments when for the revolutionary masses he is less the guarantee of the really existing party than the incarnation, all by himself, of a proletarian party that is still to come." In another he puts the victims of the twentieth-century revolutionary movements in cold-blooded perspective:

> What about the violence, often so extreme? The hundreds of thousands [*sic*] of dead? The persecutions, especially against intellectuals? One will say the same thing about them as about all those acts of violence that, to this very day, have marked the History of every somewhat expansive attempt to practice a free politics.... The theme of total emancipation, practiced in the present, in the enthusiasm of the absolute present, is always situated beyond Good and Evil.... Extreme violence is therefore the correlate of extreme enthusiasm, because it is in effect a question of the transvaluation of all values.... Morality is a residue of the old world.

After many thousands of the victims of the Vietcong escaped on their rafts into the South China Sea in the mid-1970s, and millions (not hundreds of thousands) were butchered in Cambodia, the French romance with revolution seemed to end. During the following two decades the last surviving Maoists like Badiou lived in interior exile while the political debate revolved around human rights, multiculturalism, and neoliberalism. In the new century, though, as a more radical leftism returned, Badiou made a comeback. Today he finds an audience when he denounces "capitalist-parliamentarianism, whose squalor is ever more poorly dissimulated behind the fine word 'democracy,'" or mocks race-conscious multiculturalism for causing the "Pétainization" of the French state. He has given the notion of a "neo-communism" a certain allure.

What explains Badiou's turn from Mao to Paul? We get clues from his most substantial philosophical work, *Being and Event*, which he published in 1988. Its subject is ontology (the theory of being) but it is also an earnest if abstract meditation on the idea of revolution. Though there is no God in Badiou's ontology, there are miracles, which he calls "events." Events break unpredictably into human history and establish new truths that rearrange the world and us. This sounds something like Schmitt's sovereign "decisions" except that Badiou is more of a populist, seeing a tradition of revolutionary events surging up from below, creating a chain over time. Each new event announces a new truth, but it also fulfills and justifies earlier ones in the chain. One of Pascal's enigmatic *Pensées* states that the prophecies in the Old Testament were actually false until Christian revelation made them true. Badiou, in a chapter on Pascal, makes a similar point about the history of political revolutions, suggesting that 1968 revealed and fulfilled the promise of 1917, which in turn justified 1848 and 1789, and so on. Revolution is never finished, which is why we must maintain "fidelity" to the chain of revolutionary "events," even in the darkest of times. That kind of fidelity is difficult, though, since it runs up against the evidence of our eyes. Which in turn explains why fidelity to the cause of revolution is "always the affair of an avant-garde" that understands that "what is at stake here is the militant apparatus of truth."

Like Jacob Taubes, Badiou wants to find a place for Saint Paul in the revolutionary pantheon, calling him a "poet-thinker of the event"—like the hero of 1917:

> There is currently a widespread search for a new militant figure...called upon to succeed the one installed by Lenin and the Bolsheviks at the beginning of the century.... Whence this reactivation of Paul. I am not the first to risk the comparison that makes of him a Lenin for whom Christ will have been the equivocal Marx.

For a Maoist-Leninist, Badiou is remarkably open-minded about Christianity, as long as it is seen as a revolutionary movement that upset "the previous regime of discourses." Against the Greek philosophers' pedantic demand for reasons and evidence, Jesus performed miracles and made prophecies; against Roman and Jewish law he proclaimed a universal gospel of justice and redemption based on interior faith. Jesus, for Badiou, was certainly not the Messiah, though the myth of his incarnation, crucifixion, and especially resurrection reminds us that salvation depends on "a lawless eruption."

So Badiou, like Taubes, finds the real Christian "event" in Paul's Epistle to the Romans, not in the life and teachings of Jesus. The revelation on Sinai was also a revolutionary event in history. But like a long, disreputable line of Christian theologians Badiou maintains that Jewish legalism and ethnic particularity became aggressively counterrevolutionary after the death of Christ. Real "fidelity" to the Jewish "event" demands acceptance of the new, more universal Christian event. Here Badiou's and Taubes's readings of Saint Paul diverge, to say the least. For Taubes, Paul universalized the messianic promise first given to the Hebrews, he did not abolish it. Thanks to him, we are all children of Sinai. For Badiou, Paul's militant universalism gives us a foretaste of what Kant, in a regrettable phrase, once called "the euthanasia of Judaism." The apostle, like Kant, understood that "it is imperative that universality not present itself under the aspect of a particularity," so he set out to "drag the Good News (the Gospels) out from the rigid enclosure within which its restriction to the Jewish community would confine it."

When Alain Badiou criticizes "particularity" in the context of the Epistle to the Romans, one might assume he is attack-

ing the traditional barriers to his revolutionary ideal—bourgeois individualism, private property, ethnic attachment.
Which he is. But in his journalistic essays one starts to see
that the Jews play a larger, and much darker, role in his political imagination. In 2005 Badiou published a collection of
essays titled *Circonstances 3: Portées du mot "Juif"*—"Uses
of the Word 'Jew'"—which immediately set off heated po-
lemics. In it he expresses annoyance that the word "Jew" has
become a "sacred signifier... placed in a paradigmatic position with respect to the field of values," adding, "that the
Nazis and their accomplices exterminated millions of people
they called 'Jews' does not to my mind lend any new legitimacy to the identity predicate in question."

The proximate target of this outburst is contemporary
Israel, which is charged with exploiting the Holocaust to
justify its treatment of the Palestinians and to demand repa-
rations from Western governments and individuals. *Circonstances 3* includes a wild essay on this theme by Badiou's
sometime collaborator Cécile Winter, titled "The Master-
Signifier of the New Aryans." Winter angrily informs us that
"today, in perfect continuity with Hitler's invention, the
word 'Jew' has become a transcendental signifier, an inver-
sion by which the powerful of the day turn in a profit, a
word brandished to reduce one to silence on pain of sacri-
lege." Badiou agrees, adding, "I propose that nobody any
longer accept, publicly or privately, this type of political
blackmail." In the French debate surrounding this volume
Badiou claimed to be looking out for the Jews' best interests

by criticizing Israel, given that "the principle threat to the name of Jews comes from a state calling itself Jewish." In fact, he thinks Israel may still have a universal world-historical mission, which would be to dissolve itself into a "secular and democratic Palestine" where there is "neither Arab nor Jew," and thus to become "the least racial, the least religious, and the least nationalist of states." (Apparently this is the one spot on the globe where Badiou thinks parliamentary democracy would be acceptable.) He admits, though, that this would require the rise of a "regional Mandela" in the Arab world and that the rest of the world "forget the Holocaust." In other words, a miracle.

Sentiments like these about Israel are increasingly common in Europe, but for Badiou the real problem is Jewish particularity as such. This is how he puts it in one especially distasteful passage:

> What is the desire of the petty faction that is the self-proclaimed proprietor of the word "Jew" and its usages? What does it hope to achieve when, bolstered by the tripod of the Shoah, the State of Israel, and the Talmudic Tradition—the SIT—it stigmatizes and exposes to public contempt anyone who contends that it is, in all rigor, possible to subscribe to a universalist and egalitarian sense of this word?

Translation: a petty faction stands in the way of the universal revolution, insisting on its rights and identity, setting a bad example and serving the forces of reaction. If universal truth is to shine forth, something must be done about the Jews.

Anti-Semitism, like other forms of scapegoating, is fed by historical pessimism. A certain kind of European left, which has sympathizers in American universities, has never gotten over the collapse of the revolutionary political expectations raised in the 1960s and 1970s. Anticolonial movements turned into single-party dictatorships, the Soviet model vanished, students gave up politics to pursue business careers, the party systems in Western democracies rest intact, the economies have produced wealth (unevenly shared), and the entire world is mesmerized by connectivity. There was a successful cultural revolution— feminism, gay rights, the decline of parental authority—and it has even begun spreading outside the West. But there was no political revolution and no prospect of one occurring now. What would it aim at? Who would conduct it? What would happen afterward? No one has answers to these questions and hardly anyone thinks to ask them anymore. All one finds on the (almost exclusively academic) left today is a paradoxical form of historical nostalgia, a nostalgia for "the future."

Hence the somewhat desperate search for intellectual resources to feed it. First there was the embrace of Hitler's "crown jurist" Carl Schmitt, *un mariage contre nature* if ever there were one. His idea of a hidden "sovereign decision" was borrowed to argue that liberal ideas—including ideas of neutrality and toleration—are arbitrary constructs that provide a structure for the forces of domination, aided by institutions like schools and the press. Marx's critique of ideology reached the same conclusion in the nineteenth century. But it had a fateful weakness: it depended on a materialist theory of history that could be falsified by what happens or doesn't happen in the world. After the left lost confidence in that theory, it sought support in what Marx would have called (and rightly dismissed as) idealism: an account of political domination that depended on what was *not* evident to the naked eye. Michel Foucault's theory of a "power" that, like ether, is invisible but omnipresent was a first step in that direction. The rehabilitation of Schmitt was the next: his unabashed defense of the friend–enemy distinction as the essence of "the political" helped to recover the conviction that politics is struggle, not deliberation, consultation, and compromise. Add to these notions the half-understood eschatology of Saint Paul, and faith in a miraculous redeeming revolution almost seems possible again. Not a revolution that issues from the forces of history, or the hard work of arguing and organizing. A revolution that arrives when you least expect it, like a thief in the night.

It is doubtful that Saint Paul's new postmodern enthusiasts would recognize that allusion to the First Epistle to the Thessalonians. Bible study is hard and requires devotion, and the new Paulines want things to be easy and exciting. And so long as one remains in an armchair there is an undeniable frisson to be had in reading a clever defense of Lenin or Mao or Pol Pot, and a satisfaction to be found in discovering sophisticated reasons for singling out the Jews. One can even feel active again by signing an online petition calling for a boycott of Israeli academics and their institutions. But these are literary experiences, not political ones. They provoke a very old political romanticism that longs to live life on more dramatic terms than those offered by bourgeois society, to break out and feel the hot pulse of passion, to upset the petty laws and conventions that crush the human spirit and pay the rent. We recognize this longing and know how it has shaped modern consciousness and politics, often at great cost. But its patron saint is not Paul of Tarsus. It is Emma Bovary.

Events

PARIS, JANUARY 2015

*A man cannot be angry at his own time without
suffering some damage.*

—Robert Musil

ON THE MORNING of January 7, 2015, two French Muslim
terrorists, Saïd and Chérif Kouachi, infiltrated the Paris offices of the satirical newspaper *Charlie Hebdo* and assassinated twelve people. Before escaping they shouted that they
were avenging the Prophet Muhammad for some insulting
cartoons that the paper had published over the years. The
next morning a young policewoman was shot dead by a rad-
icalized Muslim accomplice of theirs, Amedy Coulibaly, on
a street near a Jewish school just outside the city. On January
9, heavily armed, he then entered a Parisian kosher supermarket and killed four shoppers before taking the rest hos-
tage. Later that afternoon police simultaneously attacked
the supermarket and the Kouachis' hideout northeast of
Paris, killing all three terrorists. On Sunday, January 11,

demonstrations in honor of the victims were held across France, with more than a million and a half marching in Paris alongside forty-four world leaders.

The killings provoked more horror than surprise. Political Islamism had been at the center of French attention for at least two years. In 2012 a terrorist assassinated three Muslim French soldiers in southwest France, then a teacher and three students in a Jewish school. Throughout 2014 stories emerged of young people across France leaving to wage jihad in Syria: well over a thousand by the end of the year, a large portion of them recent converts and a surprising number of them young girls. By the fall videos surfaced of French jihadists participating in executions carried out by the Islamic State of Iraq and Syria (ISIS), and in October another video appeared of the beheading of a French mountain guide in Algeria. Then, two weeks before the January attacks, there were three cases of unstable Muslim men trying to kill people while crying *allahu akbar*, one by attacking three policeman with a knife, the others by driving into crowded outdoor Christmas markets in provincial cities. Given all this, it was not difficult after the January events to convince oneself that "all the signs were there" and that someone must have been culpable for ignoring them.

The controversy that followed was not a total surprise either. Ever since three pious Muslim girls were suspended from a French school in 1989 for refusing to remove their head scarves, a culture war over the place of Islam in French society had been simmering. Every few years an isolated incident—the serving of halal food in a school, riots erupting in a housing project, a mosque or synagogue being attacked, the right-wing National Front winning a local election— would revive the conflict. The Paris massacres did that again, in a major way. The intense public debate that followed was familiar. Journalists and politicians on the left were quick to declare that the attacks had "nothing to do with Islam" and warned against blaming the victims of France's failed economic and social policies. Critics on the right charged them with ignoring the present danger of political Islamism, immigration, and multiculturalism.

But then new voices were heard. They came from the right but spoke in resonant prophetic tones about the course of world history, not just about the recent past. To understand the present crisis, they said, one must go much further back—back to the two world wars, back to the rise and fall of the Third Republic, back to Napoleon, back to the French Revolution, even back to the Enlightenment or the Middle Ages. Focusing on this or that government policy, this or that reform, is to remain blind to the scale of the calamity. We no longer control our destiny: that is the truth of the matter. The situation in which we find ourselves is the foreseeable result of disastrous political and culture mistakes that set France, and perhaps the whole of Western civilization, on the path toward a catastrophe long ago. And now the reckoning has come.

Arguments like these have not been heard in France for

some time. There once was an important intellectual tradition of cultural despair running back to the French Revolution, which included some of France's most important writers, from Joseph de Maistre and Chateaubriand in the nineteenth century down to Maurice Barrès and Céline in the twentieth. But after World War II this stream of thought, now associated with fascism and the Shoah, fell into disgrace. It was still permissible for a French writer to be a conservative but not a reactionary, and certainly not a reactionary with a theory of history that condemned what everyone else considered to be modern progress. Today it is permissible. Over the past quarter-century, French society has undergone changes that almost no one is happy with, and neither left-leaning intellectuals nor centrist politicians seem capable of addressing them satisfactorily. The new reactionaries sensed an opportunity and now they are finding a public that experiences a rush of recognition when reading their books, and liberation from a sense of being misunderstood. It is to two of these writers in particular that tens of thousands of French readers turned to make sense of the dramatic events of January 2015.

One was the journalist Éric Zemmour. A few months before the Paris attacks Zemmour published a book, *Le Suicide français*, that offered a grandiose, apocalyptic vision of the decline of France in which French Muslims play a central part.* It became the second-best-selling book of 2014, and

---

Le Suicide français (Paris: Albin Michel, 2014).

the most argued over. Zemmour's incendiary comments about Islam earned him death threats, and immediately after the massacres the French government placed him under police protection. The other, and more important, figure was Michel Houellebecq, by any measure France's most significant contemporary writer. His latest novel —which in a bizarre twist of fate was published on the morning of the *Charlie Hebdo* murders—revolves around an Islamic political party coming to power in France in the near future and contains speculations about how the West's decline since the Middle Ages prepared this momentous event. Houellebecq gave it the shockingly blunt title *Submission.** Though the book appeared in stores only hours before the massacre, the Socialist prime minister Manuel Valls, in his first interview after the attacks, felt obliged to denounce its author, saying that "France is not Michel Houellebecq. It is not intolerance, hate, and fear." Yet it was Houellebecq who became the object of hate and, like Zemmour, had to be given around-the-clock police protection

I happened to be living in Paris and working on the present book when the terrorist attacks took place. In the weeks that followed I published several articles on the events in *The New York Review of Books*, including one on Zemmour and another on Houellebecq. Afterward I was struck by the affinities between these contemporary writers and the figures I discuss here in earlier chapters. I have chosen to include the

---

*Soumission (Paris: Flammarion, 2015); translated into English by Lorin Stein (Farrar, Straus and Giroux, 2015).

pieces here in something close to their original form in order to convey some of the intensity of that moment, and as a reminder that the power of historical myths to motivate political action has not diminished in our time.

SUICIDE

Éric Zemmour is less a journalist or thinker than a medium through whom the political passions of the moment pass and take on form. The son of North African Jews, he began his career writing editorials for the conservative newspaper *Le Figaro*, then started appearing on television and radio where he would give intelligent and unpredictable commentary on the issues of the day. Though clearly on the right, he seemed like a fresh, affable voice, an *épateur* of the Voltairean sort in a new, McLuhan-cool style. By 2014 that Zemmour was no more. He had become an omnipresent Jeremiah who telegraphed the same message, day in and day out, on all available media: *France awake! You have been betrayed and your country has been stolen from you.* He is not a thuggish populist of the sort the National Front attracts, though. He is well educated, literary, stylish, light on his feet, a happy warrior who never raises his voice even when delivering bad news. And in *Le Suicide français* there is a lot of it.

It is a steamroller of a book. There are seventy-nine short chapters, each devoted to a date supposedly marking France's decline. Zemmour does not transform them into a continuous narrative or even try to explain how they are connected. The connections are meant to be felt; he is a master of affect. Revisiting so many Stations of the French Cross sounds unbearable, but it is a testament to his skill as a writer and slyness as a polemicist that the book works.

The list of catastrophes and especially betrayals is long: birth control, abandonment of the gold standard, speech codes, the Common Market, no-fault divorce, poststructuralism, denationalizing important industries, abortion, the euro, Muslim and Jewish communitarianism, gender studies, surrendering to American power in NATO, surrendering to German power in the EU, surrendering to Muslim power in the schools, banning smoking in restaurants, abolishing conscription, aggressive antiracism, laws defending illegal immigrants, and the introduction of halal food in schools. The list of traitors is shorter but just as various: feminists, left-wing journalists and professors, neoliberal businessmen, anti-neoliberal activists, cowardly politicians, the educational establishment, European bureaucrats, and even coaches of professional soccer teams who have lost control of their players.

Some of the chapters are, as the French say, *hallucinants*— unhinged. The ones on Vichy, where he claims that the collaborationist government was actually trying to save French Jews, make him sound like a mere crank. But in the others he scores enough genuine points that a sympathetically inclined reader will soon be prepared to follow him into more dubious territory. He is not the sort of demagogue who nails his theses to the door and declares, "Here I stand, I can do no other." He is more fluid, his positions and arguments constantly being refreshed, like a web page, with new facts and fantasies. This creates a trap for his critics, who have obligingly jumped in. Not content to expose his exaggerations and fabrications, their instinct—a deep one on the French left since the days of the Popular Front—is to denounce anything someone on the right says, so as not to give comfort to the enemy. Their thinking is: if it is four o'clock, and Éric Zemmour says it is four o'clock, it is our duty to say it is three o'clock. Which guarantees that twice a day he will be able to look at his sympathizers and say, "You see what I mean?"

Zemmour's views are simply too eclectic to be labeled and dismissed *tout court*. And they can be surprising. Like everyone on the French right, he is a self-declared patriot nostalgic for national grandeur, and his prose turns purple whenever he quotes from de Gaulle's speeches or recounts the triumphs of Napoleon. But high on his list of national traitors is the French business class. He scolds CEOs who have outsourced jobs or planted box stores in exurban areas, effectively killing commerce in small towns and villages, whose streets have emptied, leaving only juvenile delinquents. He charges bankers and financiers with betraying workers and the nation by pushing for full European integration and abandoning the French franc. He makes much of the fact that, as others have noted, the images on the euro currency lack any historical or geographical references. One sees only bridges that connect nowhere with nowhere, and architectural elements that float in vacant space—apt metaphors for what has happened to the nation-state in Europe. The Revolution, which freed France to determine its own collective destiny, has finally been reversed by Brussels. "The aristocratic Europe of the past and the technocratic oligarchy of today have finally gotten their revenge on the incorrigible French."

Arguments like these can also be found in the left-wing antiglobalization pamphlets that fill the tables of French bookstores today. But Zemmour tosses them into a mix with more nativist right-wing arguments, like his attacks on the Sixties generation for promoting radical feminism and immigration, which he sees as connected. Ever since their loss in the Franco-Prussian War, which was ascribed to cultural and physical weakness, the French have been obsessed with their birthrate. Today it is relatively high by European standards, but appears—the government refuses to collect statistics on ethnicity—to be sustained by higher rates among families of North and Central African immigrant "stock." This has become a major obsession on the radical right, whose literature is full of predictions of an imminent *grand remplacement* that will silently turn France into a Muslim country through demographic inertia. Zemmour never mentions this theory but is clearly sympathetic to it. Due to feminism, he implies, the wombs of white women have shriveled up. And due to multiculturalism, the flood of fertile immigrants is allowed to continue. This is one more reason why French Muslims should be considered, as he has taken to saying, *"un peuple dans le peuple"*—a classic motif of European anti-Semitism that he has readapted to meet the present danger.

The French term for multiculturalism is *antiracisme*, and its history is wrapped up with the development—and decline—of the left. Former '68ers like Pascal Bruckner and Alain Finkielkraut have long argued that left-wing activists made a disastrous mistake in the 1970s by abandoning the traditional working class and turning toward identity politics. Deserted, the workers turned to the National Front and adopted its xenophobia; in response, the left formed organizations that defended immigrants and fended off any criticism of their mainly Muslim culture. The classic picture of a France that could and should turn peasants and immigrants into equal citizens was replaced by the picture of a racist nation that after repressing its colonial subjects abroad consigned them to an underclass at home. By now, so the argument goes, this antiracism is the central dogma of mainstream politics, and has stifled the will to integrate Muslims from immigrant backgrounds into French society, with disastrous results—first and foremost for Muslim youth.

But Zemmour does not give a damn about his Muslim fellow citizens, as becomes clear the deeper one gets into *Le Suicide français*. He has contempt for them—and wants his readers to as well. It is one thing to say that the antiracist rhetoric of victimization has blinded the French to the real threat of fundamentalist Islam brewing in the poor urban areas. It is quite another to dismiss out of hand, as Zemmour does, the enormous independent effects of poverty, segregation, and unemployment in making people in those areas feel hopeless, cut off, angry, and contemptuous of republican pieties. The list of policies that contribute to these conditions—and, if changed, might help to ease them—is long. And France could change them while at the same time policing the streets, maintaining authority in the classrooms, and teaching the republican values of laicity, democracy, and public duty—which one would think Zemmour would favor. But for a demagogue like him it is important to convince readers that the rot is too deep, the traitors too numerous, the Muslims too hopeless for a patchwork of measures to have any effect. To follow his suicide metaphor, it would be like devising an exercise regimen for a patient on life support. On the book's last page we read that "France is dying, France is dead." There is no final chapter on what is to be done to revive it. He leaves that to his readers' no doubt vivid imaginations.

Successful ideologies follow a certain trajectory. They are first developed in narrow sects whose adherents share obsessions and principles, and see themselves as voices in the wilderness. To have any political effect, though, these groups must learn to work together. That's difficult for obsessive, principled people, which is why at the political fringes one always finds little factions squabbling futilely with each other. But for an ideology to really reshape politics it must cease being a set of principles and become instead a vaguer general outlook that new information and events only strengthen. You really know when an ideology has matured when every event, present and past, is taken as confirmation of it. The French right, with Éric Zemmour's help, is advancing on this trajectory today. *Le Suicide français* gives readers a common set of enemies; it provides a calendar of their crimes; it confirms a suspicion that there must be some connection among those crimes; and it stirs in them an outraged hopelessness—which in contemporary politics is much more powerful than hope. All this at a time when the country is trying to wrap its collective mind around one of the great tragedies and challenges in its recent history.

Yes, the publication of *Le Suicide français* was well timed, at least for its author. For France, not so much.

SUBMISSION

Michel Houellebecq's *Submission* met an unfortunate fate. Éric Zemmour's *succès de scandale* in the fall of 2014 ensured that his novel would be subjected to intense scrutiny. So was the fact that in previous novels and in public comments Houellebecq had made highly critical remarks about Islam, one of which provoked a court case. But the astonishing, almost unimaginable, fact that the book appeared the very day of the *Charlie Hebdo* massacre has meant that for now *Submission* is being read through the prism of current events. It will take some time for the French to appreciate *Submission* for the strange and surprising thing that it is.

Houellebecq has created a new genre—the dystopian conversion tale. *Submission* is not the story some expected of an armed coup d'état, and no one in it expresses hatred or even contempt of Muslims. At one level it is simply about a man who through suffering and indifference finds himself slouching toward Mecca. At another level, though, it is about a civilization that after centuries of a steady, almost imperceptible sapping of inner conviction finds itself doing the same thing. The literature of civilizational decline, to which Zemmour's *Le Suicide français* is a minor contribution, is typically brash and breathless. Not so *Submission*. There is not even drama here—no clash of spiritual armies, no martyrdom, no final conflagration. Stuff just happens, as in all Houellebecq's fiction. All one hears at the end is a bone-chilling sigh of collective relief. The old has passed away; behold, the new has come. Whatever.

François, the main character of *Submission*, is a mid-level literature professor at the Sorbonne who specializes in the work of the Symbolist novelist J. K. Huysmans. He is, like all Houellebecq's protagonists, what the French call *un pauvre type*, a loser. He lives alone in a modern apartment tower, teaches his courses but has no friends at the university, and returns home to frozen dinners, television, and porn. Most years he manages to pick up a student and start a relationship, which ends when the girl breaks it off over summer vacation with a laconic letter that always begins, "I've met someone." He is clueless about his times. He doesn't understand why his students are so eager to get rich, or why journalists and politicians are so hollow, or why everyone, like him, is so alone. He believes that "only literature can give you that sensation of contact with another human spirit," but no one else cares about it. His sometime girlfriend Myriam genuinely loves him but he can't respond, and when she leaves to join her parents, who have emigrated to Israel because they feel unsafe in France, all he can think to say is: "There is no Israel for me." Prostitutes, even when the sex is great, only deepen the hole he is in.

We are in 2022 and a presidential election is about to take place. All the smart money is on the National Front's Marine Le Pen winning the primary, forcing the other parties to form a coalition to stop her. The wild card in all this is a new, moderate Muslim party called the Muslim Brotherhood that by now attracts about a fifth of the electorate, about as many as the Socialists do. The party's founder and president, Mohammed Ben Abbes, is a genial man who gets along well with Catholic and Jewish community leaders who share his conservative social views, and also with business types who like his advocacy of economic growth. Foreign heads of state, beginning with the pope, have given him their blessing. Given that Muslims make up at most 6 to 8 percent of the French population, it strains credibility to imagine such a party carrying any weight in ten years' time. But Houellebecq's thought experiment is based on a genuine insight: since the far right wants to deport Muslims, conservative politicians look down on them, and the Socialists, who embrace them, want to force them to accept gay marriage, no one party clearly represents their interests.

François only slowly becomes aware of the drama swirling around him. He hears rumors of armed clashes between radical right-wing nativist groups (which exist in France) and armed radical Islamists, but newspapers worried about rocking the multicultural boat have ceased reporting such things. At a cocktail party he hears gunfire in the distance, but people pretend not to notice and find excuses to leave, so he does too. As expected, Le Pen wins the presidential primary but the Socialists and the conservatives don't have enough votes between them to defeat her. So they decide to back Ben Abbes in the runoff, and by a small margin France elects its first Muslim president. Ben Abbes decides to let the other parties divide up the ministries, reserving for the Muslim Brotherhood only the education portfolio. He, unlike his coalition partners, still understands that a nation can be transformed by what happens in classrooms.

Apart from the schools, very little seems to happen at first. But over the next months François starts to notice small things, beginning with how women dress. Though the government has established no dress code, he sees fewer skirts and dresses on the street, and more baggy pants and shirts that hide the body's contours. It seems that non-Muslim women have spontaneously adopted the style to escape the sexual marketplace that Houellebecq describes so chillingly in his other novels. Youth crime declines, as does unemployment when women begin to leave the workforce, taking advantage of new family subsidies to care for their children. François thinks he sees a new social model developing before his eyes, inspired by a religion he knows little about, and which he imagines has the polygamous family at its center. Men have different wives for sex, childbearing, and affection; the wives pass through all these stages as they age, but never have to worry about being abandoned. They are always surrounded by their children, who have lots of siblings and feel loved by their parents, who never divorce. François, who lives alone and has lost contact with his parents, is impressed. His fantasy (and perhaps Houellebecq's) is not really the colonial one of the erotic harem. It is closer to what psychologists call the "family romance."

The university is a different story. After the Muslim Brotherhood comes to power, François, along with all other non-Islamic teachers, is prematurely retired with a full pension. Satisfied with the money, indifferent, or afraid, the faculty does not protest. A golden crescent is placed atop the Sorbonne gate and pictures of the Kaaba line the walls of the once-grim university offices, now restored with the money of Gulf sheikhs. The Sorbonne, François muses, has reverted to its medieval roots, back to the time of Abélard and Heloïse. The new university president, who replaced the female professor of gender studies who had presided over the Sorbonne, tries to woo him back with a better job at triple the pay, if he is willing to go through a pro forma conversion. François is polite but has no intention of doing so.

His mind is elsewhere. Since Myriam's departure he has sunk to a level of despair unknown even to him. After passing yet another New Year's alone he starts sobbing one night, seemingly without reason, and can't stop. Soon after, ostensibly for research purposes, he decides to spend some time in the Benedictine abbey in southern France where his hero Huysmans spent his last years after having abandoned his dissolute life in Paris and converted to mystical Catholicism. Houellebecq has said that originally the novel was to concern a man's struggle, loosely based on Huysmans's own, to embrace Catholicism after exhausting all the modern world had to offer. It was to be called *La Conversion* and Islam did not enter in. But he just could not make Catholicism work for him, and François's experience in the abbey sounds like Houellebecq's own as a writer, in a comic register. He only lasts two days there because he finds the sermons puerile, sex is taboo, and they won't let him smoke.

And so he heads off to the town of Rocamadour in southwest France, the impressive "citadel of faith" where medieval pilgrims once came to worship before the basilica's statue of the Black Madonna. François is taken with the statue and keeps returning, not sure quite why, until:

I felt my individuality dissolve....I was in a strange state. It seemed the Virgin was rising from her base and growing larger in the sky. The baby Jesus seemed ready to detach himself from her, and I felt that all he had to do was raise his right arm and the pagans and idolaters would be destroyed, and the keys of the world restored to him.

But when it is over he chalks the experience up to hypoglycemia and heads back to his hotel for *confit de canard* and a good night's sleep. The next day he can't repeat what happened. After half an hour of sitting he gets cold and heads back to his car to drive home. When he arrives he finds a letter informing him that in his absence his estranged mother had died alone and been buried in a pauper's grave.

It's in this state that François happens to run into the university president, Robert Rediger, and finally accepts an invitation to talk. Rediger is a marvelous creation—part Mephisto, part Grand Inquisitor, part shoe salesman. His speeches are psychologically brilliant and yet wholly transparent. The name is a macabre joke: it refers to Robert Redeker, a French philosophy teacher who received credible death threats after publishing an article in *Le Figaro* in 2006 calling Islam a religion of hate, violence, and obscurantism—and who has been living ever since under constant police protection. President Rediger is his exact opposite: a smoothie who writes sophistical books defending Islamic doctrine, and has risen in the academic ranks through flattery and influence-peddling. It is his cynicism that, in the end, makes it possible for François to convert.

To set the trap Rediger begins with a confession. It turns out that as a student he began on the radical Catholic right, though he spent his time reading Nietzsche rather than the Church Fathers. Secular humanistic Europe disgusted him. In the 1950s it had given up its colonies out of weakness of will and in the 1960s generated a decadent culture that told people to follow their bliss as free individuals, rather than do their duty, which is to have large, churchgoing families. Unable to reproduce, Europe then opened the gates to large-scale immigration from Muslim countries, Arab and black, and now the streets of French provincial towns look like souks. Integrating such people was never in the cards; Islam does not dissolve in water, let alone in atheistic republican schools. If Europe was ever to recover its place in the world, he thought, it would have to drive out these infidels and return to the true Catholic faith.

But Rediger took this kind of thinking a step further than Catholic xenophobes do. At a certain point he couldn't ignore how much the Islamists' message overlapped with his own. They, too, idealized the life of simple, unquestioning piety and despised modern culture and the Enlightenment that spawned it. They believed in hierarchy within the family, with wives and children there to serve the father. They, like he, hated diversity—especially diversity of opinion—and saw homogeneity and high birthrates as vital signs of civilizational health. And they quivered with the eros of violence. All that separated him from them was that they prayed on rugs and he prayed at an altar. But the more Rediger reflected, the more he had to admit that in truth European and Islamic civilizations were no longer comparable. By all the measures that really mattered, post-Christian Europe was dying and Islam was flourishing. If Europe was to have a future, it would have to be an Islamic one.

So Rediger changed to the winning side. And the victory of the Muslim Brotherhood proved that he was right to. As a former Islam specialist for the secret services also tells François, Ben Abbes is no radical Islamist dreaming of restoring a backward caliphate in the sands of the Levant. He is a modern European without the faults of one, which is why he is successful. His ambition is equal to that of the emperor Augustus: to unify the great continent again and expand into North Africa, creating a formidable cultural and economic force. After Charlemagne and Napoleon (and Hitler), Ben Abbes would be written into European history as its first peaceful conqueror. The Roman Empire lasted centuries, the Christian one a millennium and a half. In the distant future, historians will see that European modernity was just an insignificant, two-century-long deviation from the eternal ebb and flow of religiously grounded civilizations.

This impressive Spenglerian prophecy leaves François untouched; his concerns are all prosaic, like whether he can choose his wives. Still, something keeps him from submitting. As for Rediger, between sips of a fine Meursault and while his "Hello Kitty"–clad fifteen-year-old wife (one of three) brings in snacks, he goes in for the kill. As forbidden music plays in the background, he defends the Quran by appealing—in a brilliant Houellebecqian touch—to Dominique Aury's sadomasochistic novel *Story of O*. The lesson of O, he tells François, is exactly the same as that of the Holy Book: that "the summit of human happiness is to be found in absolute submission," of children to parents, women to men, and men to God. And in return, one receives life back in all its splendor. Because Islam, unlike Christianity, does not see human beings as pilgrims in an alien, fallen world, it does not see any need to escape it or remake it. The Quran is an immense mystical poem in praise of the God who created the perfect world we find ourselves in, and teaches us how to achieve happiness in it through obedience. Freedom is just another word for wretchedness.

And so François decides to convert, in what he imagines will be a short, modest ceremony at the Grande Mosquée de Paris. He does so without joy or sadness. He feels relief, just as he imagines his beloved Huysmans did when he converted to Catholicism. Things would change. He would get his wives and no longer have to worry about sex or love; he would finally be mothered. Children would be an adjustment but he would learn to love them, and they would naturally love their father. Giving up drinking would be more difficult but at least he would get to smoke and screw. So why not? His life is exhausted, and so is Europe's. It's time for a new one—any one.

Cultural pessimism is as old as human culture and has a long history in Europe. Hesiod thought that he was living in the Age of Iron; Cato the Elder blamed Greek philosophy for corrupting the young; Saint Augustine exposed the pagan decadence responsible for Rome's collapse; the Protestant reformers felt themselves to be living in the Great Tribulation; French royalists blamed Rousseau and Voltaire for the Revolution; and just about everyone blamed Nietzsche for the two world wars. *Submission* is a classic novel in this European tradition and deserves a small place in whatever category we put books like Thomas Mann's *The Magic Mountain* and Robert Musil's *The Man Without Qualities*. The parallels are enlightening. The protagonists in all three works witness the collapse of a civilization they are indifferent to, and whose degradation leaves them unmoored. Trapped by history, Mann's Hans Castorp and Musil's Ulrich have no means of escape except through transcendence. After listening to unresolvable debates over freedom and submission in his Swiss sanatorium, Hans falls in love with a tubercular Beatrice and has a mystical experience while lost in the snow. Ulrich is a cynical observer of sclerotic Hapsburg Vienna until his estranged sister reenters his life and he begins having intimations of an equally mystical "other condition" for humanity. Houellebecq blocks this vertical escape route for François, whose experiences at Rocamadour read like a parody of Hans's and Ulrich's epiphanies, a tragicomic failure to launch. All that's left is submission to the blind force that history is.

There is no doubt that Houellebecq wants us to see the collapse of modern Europe and the rise of a Muslim one as a tragedy. "It means the end," he told an interviewer, "of what is, after all, an ancient civilization." But that does not make Islam, in the novel at least, an evil religion, just a realistic one. It is not the imaginary Islam of non-Muslim intellectuals who think of it on analogy with the Catholic Church (as happens in France) or with the inward-looking faiths of Protestantism (as happens in northern Europe and the United States). Islam here is an alien and inherently expansive social force, an empire in nuce. It can be peaceful, but it has no interest in compromise or in extending the realm of human liberty. It wants to shape better human beings, not freer ones.

Houellebecq's critics have seen the novel as anti-Muslim because they assume that individual freedom is the highest human value—and have convinced themselves that the Islamic tradition agrees with them. It does not, and neither does Houellebecq. Whatever Houellebecq thinks of it, Islam is not the target of *Submission*. It serves as a device to express a recurring European worry that the single-minded pursuit of freedom—freedom from tradition and authority, freedom to pursue one's own ends—must inevitably lead to disaster.

His breakout novel, *The Elementary Particles*, concerned two brothers who suffered unbearable psychic wounds after being abandoned by narcissistic hippie parents who epitomized the Sixties. But with each new novel it has become clearer that Houellebecq thinks that the crucial historical turning point was much earlier. Our troubles, he now thinks, began with the Enlightenment attack on the organic wholeness of medieval society and the blind pursuit of technological advance. The qualities that Houellebecq projects onto Islam are no different from those that the religious right ever since the French Revolution has attributed to premodern Christendom: strong families, moral education, social order, a sense of place, a meaningful death, and, above all, the will to persist as a culture. And he shows a real understanding of people—from the radical nativist on the far right to radical Islamists—who despise the present and dream of stepping back in history to recover what they imagine was lost. All Houellebecq's characters seek escape, usually in sex, now in religion. His fourth novel, *The Possibility of an Island*, was set in a very distant future where biotechnology has made it possible to commit suicide once life becomes unbearable, and then to be refabricated as a clone with no recollection of our earlier states. That, it seems for Houellebecq, would be the best of all possible worlds: immortality without memory. Europe in 2022 has to find another way to escape the present, and "Islam" just happens to be the name of the next clone.

Michel Houellebecq is not angry. He does not have a program, and he is not shaking his fist at the nation's traitors as Éric Zemmour is. For all his knowingness about contemporary culture—the way we love, the way we work, the way we die—the focus in Houellebecq's novels is always on the historical *longue durée*. He appears genuinely to believe that France has, regrettably and irretrievably, lost its sense of self, but not because of feminism or immigration or the European Union or globalization. Those are just symptoms of a crisis that was set off two centuries ago when Europeans made a wager on history: that the more they extended human freedom, the happier they would be. For him, that wager has been lost. And so the continent is adrift and susceptible to a much older temptation, to submit to those claiming to speak for God. Who remains as remote and as silent as ever.

Afterword

THE KNIGHT AND THE CALIPH

*Say not, "Why were the former days better than
these?" For it is not from wisdom that you ask this.*

—Ecclesiastes 7:10

NOT LONG AFTER setting out on his first adventures, Don
Quixote is invited to share a frugal meal with a group of
goatherds. A little meat stew, hard cheese, plenty of wine.
When they finish, the goatherds spread out a quantity of
acorns and start cracking them open for dessert. All except
Don Quixote, who just rolls them in his hand, lost in a rev-
erie. He clears his throat. *Fortunate the age and fortunate
the times called golden by the ancients,* he tells the chewing
peasants. It was an age when nature's bounty lay there ready
to be gathered. There was no mine and thine, no farms, no
making of farm tools, no makers of farm tools. Modest
shepherdesses simply attired roamed the hills unmolested,
stopping only to hear the spontaneous, unaffected poetry of

their chaste lovers. No laws were enforced because none were needed.

That age ended. Why? The goatherds do not ask and Quixote doesn't burden them with his esoteric knowledge. He just reminds them of what they already know, which is that now maidens and even orphans are not safe from predators. When the Golden Age ended, laws became necessary; but since there were no pure hearts left to enforce them, the strong and vicious were free to terrorize the weak and good. That was why the order of knights was created in the Middle Ages, and why Quixote has resolved to revive it in modern times. The goatherds listen in "stupefied and perplexed" silence to this old man in his papier-mâché helmet. Sancho Panza, already used to his master's harangues, just keeps drinking.

Don Quixote, like Emma Bovary, has read too much. They are martyrs of the Gutenberg revolution. The Knight of the Sorrowful Face has absorbed so many tales of sublimated desire and derring-do that he can no longer make out his surroundings; Emma reads of fortunes made and lost, of maidens plucked from obscurity by dashing counts, of life as an endless ball. *She longed to travel; she longed to return to the convent. She wanted to die. And she wanted to live in Paris.* Both suffer, as we all do, from the fact that the world is not as it should be.

Mary McCarthy, though, had it wrong when she wrote that "Madame Bovary is Don Quixote in skirts." Emma's suffering is Platonic: she searches, in all the wrong places and with all the wrong people, for an ideal that is only imagined. Until the end she believes that she will get the love and recognition she deserves. Quixote's suffering is Christian. He has convinced himself that once upon a time the world really was what it was meant to be, that the ideal had been made flesh, then vanished. Having had a foretaste of paradise, his suffering is more acute than that of Emma, who longs for the improbable but not the impossible. Quixote awaits the Second Coming. His quest is doomed from the start because he is rebelling against the nature of time, which is irreversible and unconquerable. What is past is past; this is the thought he cannot bear. Chivalric literature has robbed him of irony, the armor of the lucid. Irony may be defined as the ability to negotiate the gap between the real and the ideal without doing violence to either. Quixote is under the illusion that the gap he perceives was caused by a historical catastrophe, not that it is simply rooted in life. He is a tragicomic messiah, wandering in the desert of his own imagination.

Quixote's fantasy is sustained by an assumption about history: that the past comes predivided into discrete, coherent ages. An "age," of course, is nothing more than a space between two markers that we place on the ticker tape of time to make history legible to ourselves. We do the same by carving "events" out of the chaos of experience, as Stendhal's Fabrizio del Dongo discovered in his futile search for the Battle of Waterloo. To put some order in our thinking, we must impose a rough-and-ready order on the past. We speak metaphorically of the "dawn of an age" or "the end of an era" without meaning that at some precise moment we crossed a border. When the past is remote, we are especially aware of what we are doing and nothing seems particularly at stake if, say, we move the boundaries of the Pleistocene epoch or the Stone Age forward or back a millennium. The distinctions are there to serve us, and when they don't we revise them or ignore them. In principle, what taxonomy is to biology, chronology should be to history.

But the closer we get to the present, and the more our distinctions concern society, the more charged chronology becomes. This is also true of taxonomy. The concept of race has one resonance when it is applied to plants, another when applied to human beings. The danger in the latter is reification. That happens when to make sense of reality we develop a concept to help sort things out (the "Aryan" linguistic group, for example), then subsequently declare it to be a fact inscribed in reality (a homogeneous "Aryan" people with a distinct culture and history). We are learning not to do that with race, but when it comes to understanding history we are still incorrigibly reifying creatures.

The urge to divide time into ages seems embedded in our imaginations. We notice that the stars and the seasons follow regular cycles and that human life follows an arc from nothingness to maturity, then back to nothingness. For civilizations ancient and modern this movement in nature provided irresistible metaphors for describing cosmological, sacred, and political change. But as metaphors age and migrate from the poetic imagination to social myth they harden into certainties. One need not have read Kierkegaard or Heidegger to know the anxiety that accompanies historical consciousness, that inner cramp that comes when time lurches forward and we feel ourselves catapulted into the future. To relax that cramp we tell ourselves we actually know how one age has followed another since the beginning. This white lie gives us hope of altering the future course of events, or at least of learning how to adapt to them. There even seems to be solace in thinking that we are caught in a fated history of decline, so long as we can expect a new turn of the wheel, or an eschatological event that will carry us beyond time itself.

Epochal thinking is magical thinking. Even the greatest minds succumb to it. For Hesiod and Ovid the "ages of man" was an allegory, but for the author of the Book of Daniel the four kingdoms destined to rule the world were a prophetic certainty. Christian apologists from Eusebius to Bossuet saw God's providential hand shaping distinct ages marking the preparation, revelation, and spread of the Gospel. Ibn Khaldun, Machiavelli, and Vico thought they had discovered the mechanism by which nations rise from rude beginnings before reaching their peak, decaying into luxury and literature, then returning cyclically to their origins. Hegel divided the history of nearly every human endeavor—politics, religion, art, philosophy—into a snaking temporal web of triads within triads. Heidegger spoke elliptically about "epochs in the history of Being" that are opened and closed by a destiny beyond human understanding (though it sometimes leaves signs, like the swastika). Even our minor academic prophets of the postmodern, by using the prefix *post-*, can't seem to overcome the compulsion to divide one age from another. Or to consider their own to be the culminating one, in which all cats are finally revealed to be gray.

Narratives of progress, regress, and cycles all assume a mechanism by which historical change happens. It might be the natural laws of the cosmos, the will of God, the dialectical development of the human mind or of economic forces. Once we understand the mechanism, we are assured of understanding what really happened and what is to come. But what if there is no such mechanism? What if history is subject to sudden eruptions that cannot be explained by any science of temporal tectonics? These are the questions that arise in the face of cataclysms for which no rationalization seems adequate and no consolation seems possible. In response an apocalyptic view of history develops that sees a rip in time that widens with each passing year, distancing us from an age that was golden or heroic or simply normal. In this vision there really is only one event in history, the *kairos* separating the world we were meant for from the world we must live in. That is all we can know, and must know, about the past.

Apocalyptic history itself has a history, which stands as a record of human despair. The expulsion from Eden, the destruction of the First and Second Temples, the crucifixion of Jesus, the sack of Rome, the murders of Hussein and Ali, the

Crusades, the fall of Jerusalem, the Reformation, the fall of Constantinople, the English Civil Wars, the French Revolution, the American Civil War, World War I, the Russian Revolution, the abolition of the caliphate, the Shoah, the Palestinian Nakba, "the Sixties," September 11—all these events have been inscribed in collective memories as definitive breaches in history. For the apocalyptic imagination, the present, not the past, is a foreign country. That is why it is so inclined to dream of a second event that will blow open the doors of paradise. Its attention is fixed on the horizon as it awaits the Messiah, the Revolution, the Leader, or the end of time itself. Only an apocalypse can save us now: in the face of catastrophe this morbid conviction can appear to be simple common sense. But throughout history it has also provoked extravagant hopes that were inevitably disappointed, leaving those who held them even more desolate. The doors to the Kingdom remained shut, and all that was left was memory of defeat, destruction, and exile. And fantasies of the world we have lost.

For those who have never experienced defeat, destruction, or exile there is an undeniable charm to loss. An alternative travel agency in Romania offers what it calls a "Beautiful Decay Tour" of Bucharest that gives the visitor an overview of the post-Communist urban landscape—buildings full of rubble and broken glass, abandoned factories invaded by local grasses, that sort of thing. Online reviews are effusive.

Young American artists, feeling unappreciated in gentrified New York, are now moving to Detroit, America's Bucharest, to feel the grit once more in their teeth. English gentlemen succumbed to something similar in the nineteenth century, buying up deserted abbeys and country houses where they shivered on the weekends. For romantics, the decay of the ideal is the ideal.

La nostalgie de la boue is alien to history's victims. Finding themselves on the other side of the chasm separating past and present, some recognize their loss and turn to the future, with hope or without it: the camp survivor who never mentions the number tattooed on his arm, playing with his grandchildren on a Sunday afternoon. Others remain at the edge of the chasm and watch the lights recede on the other side, night after night, their minds ricocheting between anger and resignation: the aged White Russians sitting around a samovar in a *chambre de bonne*, the heavy curtains drawn, tearing up as they sing the old songs. Some, though, become idolaters of the chasm. They are obsessed with taking revenge on whatever demiurge caused it to open up. Their nostalgia is revolutionary. Since the continuity of time has already been broken, they begin to dream of making a second break and escaping from the present. But in which direction? Should we find our way back to the past and exercise our right of return? Or should we move forward to a new age inspired by the golden one? Rebuild the Temple or found a kibbutz?

The politics of nostalgia are about nothing but such questions. After the French Revolution, dispossessed aristocrats and clergy camped along the French border confident that they would return home shortly and set the furniture aright. They had to wait a quarter-century, and by then France no longer was what it had been. The Restoration wasn't one. Yet nostalgic Catholic monarchism remained a strong current in French politics up until World War II, when movements like the Action Française were finally disgraced for collaborating with Vichy. Small groups of sympathizers still exist, though, and the newspaper *Action Française* continues to appear on newsstands, like a specter, every two weeks. The Germans' defeat in World War I pushed Adolf Hitler in the opposite direction. He might have projected the image of a restored old Germany of conservative villages nestled in Bavarian valleys, populated by Hans Sachses who could sing and fight. Instead he spoke of a new Germany inspired by the ancient tribes and the Roman legions, now riding Panzer tanks unleashing storms of steel and ruling over a hypermodern industrial Europe cleansed of Jews and Bolsheviks. Forward into the past.

Apocalyptic historiography never goes out of style. Today's American conservatives have perfected a popular myth of how the nation emerged from World War II strong and virtuous, only to become a licentious society governed by a menacing secular state after the Nakba of the Sixties. They are divided over how to respond. Some want to return to an idealized traditional past; others dream of a libertarian future where frontier virtues will be reborn and Internet speeds will be awesome. Things are more serious in Europe, especially in the east, where old maps of Greater Serbia in cold storage since 1914 were pulled out and posted on the Internet as soon as the Berlin Wall fell, and Hungarians began retelling old tales about how much better life was when there weren't so many Jews and Gypsies around. Things are critical in Russia, where all problems are now attributed to the cataclysmic breakup of the USSR, which allows Vladimir Putin to sell dreams of a restored empire blessed by the Orthodox Church and sustained by pillage and vodka.

But it is in the Muslim world that belief in a lost Golden Age is most potent and consequential today. The more deeply one reads into the literature of radical Islamism, the more one appreciates the appeal of the myth. It goes something like this. Before the arrival of the Prophet the world was in an age of ignorance, the *jahiliyya*. The great empires were sunk in pagan immorality, Christianity had developed a life-denying monasticism, and the Arabs were superstitious drinkers and gamblers. Muhammad was then chosen as the vessel of God's final revelation, which uplifted all individuals and peoples who accepted it. The companions of the Prophet and the first few caliphs were impeccable conveyors of the message and began to construct a new society based on divine law. But soon, astonishingly soon, the élan of this founding generation was lost. And it has never been recovered. In Arab lands conquerors came and went—Umayyads,

Abbasids, Christian Crusaders, Mongols, Turks. When believers remained faithful to the Quran there was some semblance of justice and virtue, and there were a few centuries when the arts and sciences progressed. But success always brought luxury, and luxury bred vice and stagnation. The will to impose God's sovereignty died.

At first, the arrival of the colonial powers in the nineteenth century appeared to be just another Western Crusade. But in fact it presented a wholly new and far graver challenge to Islam. The medieval Crusaders wanted to conquer Muslims militarily and convert them from one religion to another. The modern colonizers' strategy was to weaken Muslims by converting them away from religion altogether and imposing on them an immoral secular order. Rather than meet holy warriors on the battlefield, the new Crusaders simply held out the trinkets of modern science and technology, mesmerizing their foes. If you abandon God and usurp His legitimate rule over you, they purred, all this will be yours. Very soon the talisman of secular modernity did its work and Muslim elites became fanatics of "development," sending their children—including girls—to secular schools and universities, with predictable results. They were encouraged in this by the tyrants who ruled over them with the West's support and at its bidding suppressed the faithful.

All these forces—secularism, individualism, materialism, moral indifference, tyranny—have now combined to bring about a new *jahiliyya* that every faithful Muslim must struggle against, just as the Prophet did at the dawn of the seventh century. He did not compromise, he did not liberalize, he did not democratize, he did not pursue development. He spoke God's word and instituted His law, and we must follow his sacred example. Once that is accomplished, the glorious age of the Prophet and his companions will return for good. *Inshallah.*

There is little that is uniquely Muslim in this myth. Even its success in mobilizing the faithful and inspiring acts of extraordinary violence has precedents in the Crusades and in Nazi efforts to return to Rome by way of Walhalla. When the Golden Age meets the Apocalypse the earth begins to quake.

What is striking is how few antibodies contemporary Islamic thought has against this myth, for reasons historical and theological. Among the jewels of wisdom and poetry in the Quran one also encounters a degree of insecurity, unusual in sacred texts, about Islam's place in history. From the very first few suras we are invited to share Muhammad's frustration at being rebuffed by Jews and Christians, whose prophetic legacy he came to fulfill, not abolish. No sooner does the Prophet begin his mission than history goes a little off course and an adjustment has to be made for "peoples of the Book" blind to the treasure laid before them. Saint Paul confronted a similar challenge in his epistles, where he counseled peaceful coexistence among pagan Christians, Jewish Christians, and Jewish non-Christians. Some Quranic verses are generous and tolerant about resistance to the Prophet. Far more are not. The Quran has an unmistakable chip on its shoulder about its belatedness that can be easily exploited by those who have chips on their shoulders about the present. Untrained readers ignorant of the deep intellectual traditions of Quranic interpretation, who for whatever reason feel or can be made to feel angry about their conditions of life, are easy prey for those who would use the Quran to teach that historical grudges are sacred. From there it is not a large step to begin thinking that historical revenge is sacred, too.

Once the butchery ends, as it eventually must, through exhaustion or defeat, the pathos of political Islamism will deserve as much reflection as its monstrosity. One almost blushes to think of the historical ignorance, the misplaced piety, the outsize sense of honor, the impotent adolescent posturing, the blindness to reality, and fear of it, that lay behind the murderous fever. The pathos of Quixote is quite different. The Knight of the Sorrowful Face is absurd but noble, a suffering saint stranded in the present who leaves those he meets improved, if slightly bruised. He is a flexible fanatic, occasionally winking at Sancho Panza as if to say, *Don't worry, I'm onto myself.* And he knows when to stop. After being defeated in a mock battle arranged by friends hoping to wake him from his dreams, he renounces chivalry, falls ill, and never recovers. Sancho tries to revive him by suggesting that they retire to the countryside and live as simple shepherds together, as in the Golden Age. But it's no use;

he meets death humbly. A triumphant, avenging Quixote is unthinkable.

The literature of radical Islamism is a nightmare version of Cervantes's novel. Those who write it feel stranded in the present, too, but have divine assurance that what is lost in time can be found in time. To God, the past is never past. The ideal society is always possible, since it once existed and there are no social conditions necessary for its realization; what has been and must be, can be. All that's lacking is faith and will. The adversary is not time itself, it is those who in every historical epoch have stood in God's way. This powerful idea is not new. Considering the conservative reactions to the revolutions of 1848, Marx wrote that in epochs of revolutionary crisis we "anxiously conjure up the spirit of the past" to comfort ourselves in the face of the unknown. He was confident, though, that such reactions were temporary and that human consciousness was destined to catch up to what was already happening in the material world. Today, when political bedtime stories seem more potent than economic forces, it is hard to share his confidence. We are only too aware that the most powerful revolutionary slogans of our age begin: *Once upon a time . . .*